Journey Back Again
Reasons to Revisit Middle-earth

Second Edition

Jensen A. Kirkendall
Jordan F. Mar
Britta E. Bunnel
Mark E. Jung
Hana Paz
Anna K. Dickinson
Jacob Bradley
Joshua Harbman
Wyatt Zeimis

Edited by Diana Pavlac Glyer
Foreword by Janet Brennan Croft

Mythopoeic Press 2022
Altadena, California, USA

© 2022 by Mythopoeic Press

Copyright Notice: Mythopoeic Press owns the copyright on the entirety of the text published here as a collective work. As a collective work, it may not be reproduced, reprinted, transmitted, or distributed in any form or by any means, whether electronic or mechanical, now known or hereafter invented, without the express written permission of the official representative of Mythopoeic Press. Authors with contributions contained in the collective work are the sole copyright owners of their own individual or jointly written essays. Written permission to reprint, reproduce, transmit or distribute any individual essay must be acquired from its author. Future publications or public use of any individual essay contained in this collective work must acknowledge its original publication here by Mythopoeic Press.

Published by Mythopoeic Press, Altadena, California, USA
www.mythsoc.org/press.htm

Mythopoeic Press is an imprint of the Mythopoeic Society. Orders may be placed through our website. For general inquiries, contact:
 press@mythsoc.org
 Editor, Mythopoeic Press
 P.O. Box 6707, Altadena, CA 91003, USA

ISBN: 978-1-887726-29-0
LCCN: 2022942589

Cover design by Caedon Spilman (photo by Tobias Keller on Unsplash)
Pre-press production by Leslie A. Donovan (Mythopoeic Press Editor), Paul Irwin,
 and Megan Kornreich
Index compiled by David Bratman

Contents

Foreword
   Janet Brennan Croft i
Preface
   Diana Pavlac Glyer iii
Abbreviations v
Epigraph vii

Introduction
   Jensen A. Kirkendall 1
Chapter 1: A Narrative Quest
   Jensen A. Kirkendall 5
Chapter 2: Unexpected Worth
   Jordan F. Mar 25
Chapter 3: The Community Quilt
   Britta E. Bunnel 37
Chapter 4: Restoring Broken Fellowship
   Mark E. Jung 57
Chapter 5: Navigating the Weight of Evil
   Hana Paz 67
Chapter 6: Making the Risky Choice
   Anna K. Dickinson 85
Chapter 7: Providence at Work
   Jacob Bradley 97
Chapter 8: An Enchanted World
   Joshua Harbman 109
Chapter 9: The Road to Recovery
   Wyatt Zeimis 123
Epilogue
   Wyatt Zeimis and Jensen A. Kirkendall 137

Works Cited 141
Acknowledgments 151
About the Contributors 153
Index 157

Foreword
Janet Brennan Croft

*J*OURNEY BACK AGAIN IS AN AMBITIOUS PROJECT: a collection which is far more than just an assortment of unrelated parts. It is a conversation in book form, where the authors of the papers work as both individuals and as a creative community, writing back and forth to each other while finding new insights to contribute to the many-decades-old field of Tolkien studies. In this they exemplify what their mentor Diana Pavlac Glyer has written about in *The Company They Keep* (2007) and *Bandersnatch* (2016): good writing is seldom a solitary endeavor, but rises to new heights when it is the deliberate product of acknowledged mutual influence, intellectual hospitality, and the ongoing conversation of a fellowship of friends. And I use the word *fellowship* deliberately, as these authors do, to evoke a central tenet of *The Lord of the Rings*: we become better and stronger as we are both challenged and supported by working together with our companions.

I have enjoyed watching this project evolve, and I find myself reminded over and over again that every first reading is a fresh beginning, to which each reader brings a unique perspective and with which they engage in a way that is theirs alone — but that these new perspectives are more fruitful when shared, discussed, and honed through interaction with others.

New observations like the ones I encountered many times in these pages can, as Wyatt Zeimis points out in his chapter, lead us to a "recovery" of our perspective on Tolkien as we look through other eyes. Sharing these "recoveries" is the boon we bring back to the community from our journeys. Jensen A. Kirkendall, for example, pulls together a list of events under the heading "Detours" that aren't usually considered together. Hana Paz marks the significance that a simple paragraph break can silently imply. Mark E. Jung shows that stewardship can subvert strict hierarchy, and Anna K. Dickinson draws our attention to a passage that I do not think I have ever seen examined in such detail before. Every chapter has some arresting point of interest in it.

As Britta E. Bunnel observes of Aragorn and Gandalf in her paper, the spirit of mentorship works both ways; those who learn from a wise mentor may also in turn inspire their mentor's own future path. With Diana Pavlac Glyer as their inspiring and inspired mentor, these contributors have entered into the long conversation of scholarship with confidence, engaging with the work that has gone before and sharing their own fresh observations (and fresh approach to working as a collective) with us. There is great potential in this rising generation of writers and their collaborative approach, and I look forward to seeing where their scholarly paths take both this fellowship and its individual members in the future.

Preface
Diana Pavlac Glyer

ONE OF MY FAVORITE PASTIMES is hiking, and I am lucky enough to live in the foothills of the San Gabriel mountains, where the weather is mild and the trails are plentiful. My favorite trail follows along the top of the ridge of the mountain range: a wide, sandy path that offers incredible views. I've seen deer along that path, and tarantulas. And I've encountered a snake or two. Although I've not yet met a bear, I've seen their enormous paw prints in the mud along the way.

I never tire of these walks, in part because I love being outside and in part because no matter how often I pull on my hiking boots and climb that hill, I always see something I've never noticed before. A small purple flower. A distant oak. A hawk catching air currents and circling above me.

Tolkien loved nature, too, and his sub-created world presents layers and layers that reflect the natural world: beauty, weather, and wildness, a field of yellow *elanor*, a bright star, a lone fox, a soaring bird. Creatures, peoples, habitats. Virtues, trials, adventures. Harmony, conflict, romance. Ideas as lofty as the philosophy of evil and as concrete and ordinary as Sam's old pots and pans.

It has been an extraordinary privilege to work alongside these nine scholars as we have journeyed together through the paths of Middle-earth. As we read and re-read *The Lord of the Rings*, we kept asking the question "What do you notice?" and "What do you see?" Working together, we made fresh discoveries at every turn.

These scholars have done their research, sure, but they have also brought their enthusiasm and courage and heart to the task. And as the editor of this book, here is what delights me more than anything: this is more than a collection of essays. These writers learned to lean on one another through every step of the process, and you will see evidence of that very fact throughout these pages. To work together at the level of reading, thinking, drafting, questioning, challenging, and revising in this way is rare. To persist in it with courage and good cheer is a blessing. And when it works, it is spectacular.

The book you hold in your hand is an invitation for you to walk alongside us, to revisit Middle-earth, and to discover details you might have missed. Enjoy.

Abbreviations

FL = *The Four Loves* by C. S. Lewis
FS = "On Fairy-stories" by J. R. R. Tolkien
H = *The Hobbit* by J. R. R. Tolkien
Letters = *The Letters of J. R. R. Tolkien*, edited by Humphrey Carpenter, with the assistance of Christopher Tolkien
LotR = *The Lord of the Rings* by J. R. R. Tolkien
Mythlore = *Mythlore: A Journal of J. R. R. Tolkien, C. S. Lewis, Charles Williams, and Mythopoeic Literature*
S = *The Silmarillion* by J. R. R. Tolkien
UT = *Unfinished Tales of Númenor and Middle-earth* by J. R. R. Tolkien
VDT = *The Voyage of the Dawn Treader* by C. S. Lewis

An unliterary man may be defined as one who reads books once only. [...] We do not enjoy a story fully at the first reading. Not till the curiosity, the sheer narrative lust, has been given its sop and laid asleep, are we at leisure to savour the real beauties. Till then, it is like wasting great wine on a ravenous natural thirst which merely wants cold wetness.

— C. S. Lewis "On Stories"

Introduction
Jensen A. Kirkendall

AFTER THEIR HARROWING EXPERIENCES in the Old Forest, Merry, Pippin, Sam, and Frodo find refuge in Tom Bombadil's house. When they first arrive, cold and shaken by the fact that a willow tree just tried to eat them, Tom does not explain the nature of the sinister Old Man Willow until they have rested. When Tom gathers them around his big chair, he answers their questions in the form of "long tales" (*LotR* I.7.129).[1] He tells them remarkable stories, sometimes singing and dancing, sometimes talking to himself, but all the while weaving together the story of the forest — with all its insects and grasses, its evil and good.

Listening to this story, the hobbits begin to "understand the lives of the Forest," seeing themselves as strangers in this land (*LotR* I.7.129). Weaving in and out of this tale is Old Man Willow, who they learn is as old as the earth and a menace older than Sauron. Tom then expands his story beyond the woods to the lands just outside of it, casting the hobbits' imaginations back to the ancient battles of the first and second ages. Eventually, he goes even further, into "strange regions" past their memory, "into times when the world was wider," when there were only Elves, and even before (*LotR* I.7.131).

This "story time" with Tom Bombadil is neither juvenile nor pointless. His tale-telling exemplifies the way stories function in Middle-earth. The hobbits are, in one sense, entertained, but this is not all. The stories give them a vision of a reality far beyond themselves. This reality is "not comfortable lore," but nonetheless leaves them "enchanted" by the wonder of the world (*LotR* I.7.129, 131). It captures their imaginations.

---

[1] This book references passages from *The Lord of the Rings* as well as the preface and appendices with this format throughout: (*LotR* Bk.Ch.p). This allows readers to locate passages, regardless of differing editions. Page numbers refer to the following edition: J. R. R. Tolkien, *The Lord of the Rings*, 50th Anniversary ed.

None of the hobbits stand up and tell Bombadil, "This is all fine and good, but these are merely stories!" In Middle-earth, it is understood that wisdom is often expressed best through the lore, history, and legends of the past. The hobbits readily discern the truth and importance of all that Tom says. This storytelling is essential. It prepares the hobbits to face not just the rest of the world but also the dark powers beyond it. It could be said that Tom tells them what they need to know by means of the very genre in which Tolkien chooses to write.

Tolkien claims that "successful Fantasy" relies upon "a sudden glimpse of the underlying reality or truth" (FS 71). He claims that this is what makes fantasy delightful. This indicates Tolkien's belief that fantasy is, first of all, meant to be enjoyed. But many are inclined to leave it at that. Fantasy tends to be relegated to fiction that is merely entertaining and recreational but not sophisticated, edifying, or of literary merit.

Journey Back Again is an attempt to expand beyond this view by example, rather than by argument. Each chapter contains a reason why *The Lord of the Rings* as a work of fantasy is not only worth reading but is worth reading many times. The underlying assumption of each chapter is what Tolkien suggests above: truth and reality run through all of Middle-earth.

To say that a work of fantasy is true and realistic is not to indicate that it is factual. Middle-earth has walking trees, wizards, and magic rings, none of which are rooted in the material world as we know it. Truth is not the same as fact. Facts are all around us, but truth is often more elusive than we realize, and good fantasy helps us see truth more clearly. An imagined world is a reshuffling of our own, a kaleidoscopic turning of things to reveal new angles, an overturning of familiar soil to give it room to take in new seed. Middle-earth is such a world.

In recollection, however, all seems simple, straightforward, and easily categorized. There are fantasy creatures who go on a journey to beat the bad guy, and they win. But as soon as you look back at the actual words on the page, deeper meaning unfolds, neat categories unravel, and seeming simplicity proves deeply complex. The magic of Middle-earth is a subtle type of enchantment, not flashy like most of us imagine it would be. Events that seem random have an alluring hint of providence about them. People are baffling, and with proper attention paid, they never fail to defy expectations. Hobbits are dismissed as insignificant, and in less than a year, they overthrow the greatest threat of their era, both abroad and at home.

These are just a few examples expanded on in this book, ultimately suggesting that Middle-earth is not as simple as, at first, it may seem. They are but a sampling of particular places to look more closely and ways to think more deeply about Tolkien's work. While doing so is not necessary for enjoying the story, this type of scholarship can stimulate new insight that ultimately leads back to the story itself.

The Lord of the Rings is capable of reorienting the imagination to better see what is true and beautiful in our own world. However, this process is, by nature, inefficient. No matter how impactful a great work of art is, this impact does not easily endure. Humans are a forgetful race. We must go back again and again, allowing Tolkien's world to refresh our vision of our world. He tells us wonderful stories and reminds us what is worth paying attention to: things like human connection, sacrificial leadership, the power of mercy, the profundity of hope, and the significance of ordinary heroes. Middle-earth warrants a second look, a lingered attention, a longer walk among its hills and mountains. Giving this extra bit of attention brings Middle-earth into focus, in both its griefs and its joys. Ultimately, this can encourage us to reconsider our own world, to honestly face the sorrow and the wonder of it all.

Chapter 1

A Narrative Quest
Jensen A. Kirkendall

DAILY LIFE WOULD BE a lot more exciting if we started referring to our weekly errands of grocery shopping and lawn mowing as quests. The word "quest" evokes a certain grandeur and loftiness most of us do not feel about our lives. Choosing to view life as a quest allows all of the ups and downs to become meaningful. The small moments, both pleasant and unpleasant, can be part of a bigger story — a story that we hope leads us to the places we want to go.

This is one of the appeals of stories. They tell us about the winding and tumultuous paths of characters as they make their way through the world. The best stories are the ones that draw us into this world, making us feel like we are walking alongside the characters, seeing what they see and feeling what they feel. After returning from these types of stories, we emerge to see our own world with a refreshed vision.[2] This vision is not always comforting, for it may indicate realities we would rather ignore, but it always has the potential to teach us something important.

The Lord of the Rings does this drawing in and refreshing of vision particularly well. Middle-earth continues to capture the imaginations of many: the characters are engaging, the road is filled with adventure, and the vibrancy of the world is captivating. However, some readers find reading *The Lord of the Rings* to be an arduous journey. It requires a degree of attention and energy that causes many to simply opt for the movies instead. Despite this challenge, the very structure and design of Tolkien's narrative make it worth reading again and again.

I propose, here at the beginning, a seemingly trivial example. Early on in the story, before Frodo would even use the word "quest" for his own journey, the narrator describes Frodo, Pippin, and Sam camping for the night on their way to Crickhollow. Suddenly, from out of the

---

[2] See Zeimis's Ch. 9 for Tolkien's idea of "recovery" as an integral function of fantasy.

woods, an unnamed, nondescript fox emerges. The narrator informs us with a direct quotation from the fox's mind that the fox found it "mighty queer" to find three hobbits out and about at night, sleeping in the woods (*LotR* I.3.72). At first, this moment seems insignificant. However, lingering on it prompts the question: why would Tolkien include the thoughts of a fox in this grand epic narrative?

Bear this question in mind, for I will return to it at the very end of this chapter, only with new vocabulary to deepen our understanding of Tolkien's work. While the rest of the chapters of *Journey Back Again* examine and evaluate themes pertaining to the content of *The Lord of the Rings*, this chapter starts with more foundational aspects regarding the narrative's form — the narrative techniques Tolkien employs in telling the story. Form and content work together to communicate the meaning of the work as a whole. The best authors employ a form that deepens their stories' meaning, communicating what they want it to on multiple levels. The content likewise becomes dependent upon the form for its meaning. This makes the form indispensable to the content, not merely a container for the plot points of the story.[3]

In his discussion of Tolkien's narrative style, Charles Moseley points out that the very first thing a reader encounters is not the content of the story but the form and style of how it is told (Moseley 41). All stories contain countless decisions concerning narrative technique. These include overarching concerns, such as tone and the order of events, as well as page-by-page decisions, such as specific metaphors and how much to describe a character.

Tolkien's narrative choices are distinct in many ways, but four storytelling techniques in particular stand out. The best way to explain these is in terms of a journey, and the perspectives, detours, discoveries, and vitality encountered along the way. These apply to both the narrative journey of *The Lord of the Rings* and any journey taken in our own lives. By courageously choosing to go beyond their beloved Shire, the hobbits encounter new perspectives from their fellow travelers, unforeseen detours in the paths they must take, invaluable discoveries about the land of Middle-earth, and the breathtaking vitality of the world they inhabit.

---

[3] Martha C. Nussbaum explains this idea well: "Style itself makes its own claims, expresses its own sense of what matters. Literary form is not separable from philosophical content, but is, itself, a part of content — an integral part, then, of the search for the statement of truth" (3).

Perspectives

The characters of the story operate as windows to view Middle-earth. The narrator of *The Lord of the Rings* narrows in on particular characters' perspectives at particular points in the narrative. The narration alternates carefully between general description and personal character perspectives. Usually, the narrator provides the perspective of the least experienced figure present.[4]

This closeness to the characters is carefully chosen to ground the reader in the narrative, provide relatability to the characters, and communicate important meanings that would otherwise be lost. The close-up perspectives are most often through the hobbits' eyes, allowing us to relate to their experience of the vast newness of wider Middle-earth.[5] These close-ups are subtle, yet influential to the reader's experience.

Pippin's experiences with the *palantír* and with Minas Tirith serve as good first examples (*LotR* III.11; V.1). Throughout these passages, Pippin serves as the focal point of the reader's attention. After the events at Isengard, the narrator describes Pippin's erratic behavior towards Gandalf and Merry, his restlessness, and eventually his theft of the *palantír* while Gandalf sleeps. Alone with Pippin and the globe, the reader watches helplessly as the hobbit engages with the mind of Sauron.

No other character's internal perspective is given during these events. It might seem more pertinent for the narrator to focus on Gandalf, Théoden, or Aragorn as they contemplate what to do about the Dark Lord. Instead, we hear about Pippin's internal emotions that seem largely petty and unwarranted. Pippin is haunted by his passing encounter with the *palantír* and uncharacteristically bitter toward Gandalf for taking it from him so abruptly (*LotR* III.11.590–91). He expresses his desire to examine it to Merry, who mostly shrugs it off and tells him to wait until morning.

---

[4] I am indebted to David Bratman for this important observation about the pattern of focalization. This observation also points to Mar's observation in Ch. 2 regarding the frequent inversions of expectation regarding what is most important in *The Lord of the Rings*.

[5] Stephen Yandell claims that Tolkien's narrator is centered on the hobbits' perspectives. He explains that the narrator is not removed, lofty, and omniscient as in *The Silmarillion*, nor is he a deeply attentive guide through the journey as in *The Hobbit*. Rather, the narrator subtly offers grounding for the reader at key moments by filtering the narrative through particular characters (389).

We see here the strong and strange influence of Sauron. His evil will is capable of twisting Pippin's mind just enough to create this uncharacteristic irritability. Merry agrees with Pippin that he would like to see the stone but is content to wait until morning. Pippin's itch seems subtly malevolent. Filtering the narration through his perspective allows us to experience this passage more intimately, creating a unique sense of how Sauron threatens the company in this moment through the seemingly least significant person present.

This theme of reorienting what is significant comes out even stronger when we rejoin Pippin in Book V as he enters Minas Tirith, the great city of Men. As is true of the whole narrative, the narrator does not communicate any of Gandalf's internal perspective on Minas Tirith but only relays what he says out loud and how he interacts with Denethor. By remaining with Pippin throughout this passage, the reader gets to experience how overwhelming the city is to a newcomer. This would not be possible if the narrator were focused on Gandalf's experience since he has been to the city many times.

After their arrival, the reader then experiences more commonplace aspects of the city. Instead of grand debates between Gandalf and Denethor or exciting battle plans, the reader witnesses a great deal of conversation between Pippin and his guide, Beregond, about such commonplace things as hobbit culture and where to get a meal.[6] Then there is some waiting for Gandalf, some wandering about the city, and a meeting with some children, including Beregond's son, Bergil, in an obscure alley of the city.

It is remarkable that these seemingly insignificant events are chosen as worth narrating. Yet, throughout these passages, Pippin has many fascinating conversations. He experiences many things that give the reader insight into the races of both Men and Hobbits. Following Pippin's experiences in this manner keeps the reader rooted in the narrative by showing the world through the eyes of a character who knows just as little as we do about the city of Minas Tirith.

---

[6] One of the most alluring aspects of Tolkien's story is how much time and effort he spends crafting supporting characters that are fleshed out and compelling with all their idiosyncrasies and cultural nuances. Farmer Maggot, Tom Bombadil, Butterbur, Quickbeam, Beregond and Bergil, Wormtongue, Éomer, Ghân-buri-Ghân: any of these characters might seem insignificant at first, but Tolkien masterfully depicts them as realistic beings who exist in Middle-earth, not just useful devices to further the narrative. They all end up playing key roles in the Quest in their own way.

A Narrative Quest

Gérard Genette calls this technique of perspective "focalization."[7] This term indicates the narrowing in of the narrator, filtering all the aspects of particular scenes through a carefully chosen character.[8] This brings us back to the discussion of form and content working together to communicate meaning. The meaning communicated in the content of the chapter is accentuated by the way it is narrated. The altering of expectations is a theme from the beginning of the narrative. It is especially evident in the conversations Pippin has in Minas Tirith (*LotR* V.1.756–69). Pippin says as much when admonishing Bergil, telling him that when he is older, he will realize "folk are not always what they seem" (*LotR* V.1.769). The focalization of the narrative through Pippin's eyes accentuates the fact that, throughout this chapter, Pippin forces people to shift their expectations about Hobbits. The content and the form work together to underscore this theme.

Another example of close-up perspective, or focalization, occurs when Merry aids Éowyn in slaying the Nazgûl. This passage demonstrates the importance of the narrator's alternation between general description and internal character perspective (*LotR* V.6.840–42). Many of the most meaningful aspects of this passage are expressed from Merry's perspective. We could not experience this scene in the same way without it.

The narrator begins the scene with lofty diction — the ornate phrase "But lo!," several archaic syntactical arrangements, and the epic depiction of Éowyn standing alone between the Nazgûl and Théoden (Hammond and Scull 562). This is contrasted with Merry's bumbling efforts to engage in the battle. The reader only receives auditory descriptions of the narrative since Merry is blinded by the paralyzing dread of the Nazgûl's presence. The reader hears Merry's thoughts as he fights nobly against this paralysis, urging himself to stand by the King. One of the key moments of the passage is when Éowyn boldly stands up to the Nazgûl, causing it to be struck with sudden silence. Immediately after this, Merry's vision returns (*LotR*

---

[7] The narration can be focalized in different ways — through the eyes of a single character for a whole chapter, shifting quickly between various characters within the same page, or only focalizing externally through dialogue and speech (Genette 189–90).

[8] For an insightful examination of this technique in connection to literary world-building in fantasy and historical fiction novels, see Allan Turner's "One Pair of Eyes: Focalisation and Worldbuilding."

V.6.841). This demonstrates that Éowyn's boldness actually does cause the Nazgûl to hesitate, thereby allowing Merry to overcome his paralysis. Focalization through Merry's eyes highlights the significance of Éowyn's bravery.

Following the dissipation of the Nazgûl, Éowyn falls unconscious, making Merry the only witness to Théoden's last words — words that absolve Merry's disobedience and affirm that any valiant heart is welcome in battle.[9] Théoden tells him not to be distressed about disobeying his orders, for "great heart will not be denied. Live now in blessedness" (*LotR* V.6.842–43). Although he speaks specifically to Merry after this, it is not a far reach to extend these words of absolution to Éowyn as forgiveness for her disobedience in joining the battle when she was commanded to remain at home (*LotR* V.2.784). Based on the way this battle is described, no one would deny Éowyn's demonstration of "great heart." Although the reader never sees them talk about Théoden's last words, Merry nevertheless becomes the carrier of potential absolution for Éowyn that Théoden could not give himself. The alternation between general description and Merry's internal perspective in this passage enriches the scene to communicate and carry even more significance than it would with simple narration.

Another example of the perspective given by focalization is Gimli's journey through the Paths of the Dead (*LotR* V.2.786–88). This is the only time the reader experiences Gimli's internal perspective. Gimli articulates his fear at the entrance to the Paths of the Dead, though everyone else remains silent. All enter, Legolas exhibiting no sign of fear at the dead spirits of Men. Gimli is irate that he, as a Dwarf, is unwilling to enter underground when an Elf is (*LotR* V.2.786).[10] The reader follows blindly with Gimli at the back of the company as he feels a growing sense of dread with every step. The narrator then

---

[9] One of the narrative techniques of *The Lord of the Rings* I do not discuss is the consistent use of paragraph breaks or section breaks within chapters. A paragraph break separates the death of the Nazgûl from the description of Merry's actions just afterward, greatly adding to the weight of this moment of victory. After the pause, the narrative does not highlight triumph but instead demonstrates Merry's shock, weariness, and concern for his fallen companions. Paz discusses the significance of paragraph breaks further in Ch. 5 in her section, "Weighing Evil in Middle-earth."

[10] Legolas's lack of fear in this section is intriguing and is partially explained by the difference in the afterlives of Elves and Men, explained in Ch. 12, "Of Men," in *The Silmarillion*, pp. 103–05.

informs the reader that there is an invisible host of spirits following the group, though Gimli cannot see it. Under his breath, Gimli wonders if Aragorn feels any fear. The reader is left to wonder this as well, for no glimpse is given into Aragorn's mind (*LotR* V.2.787). The last hour of the journey is summarized in the observation that Gimli does not remember it well, highlighting the fact that we are only getting the account through Gimli's eyes (*LotR* V.2.787).

Experiencing the Paths of the Dead in this way offers a unique experience for the reader. Gimli's discomfort emphasizes the unnatural quality of the setting, and his fear signals the reader to the invisible happenings. While it might seem more intuitive to follow Aragorn as the central figure for this chapter, Tolkien's narrator gives voice to the less expected and more relatable perspective. To see into Aragorn's mind would give the reader a great deal of information about what is going on, while being with Gimli creates suspense and intrigue regarding what will happen next.

Although subtle, the focalization throughout the narrative creates both vibrant characters and nuanced meaning in the story. There are countless other examples that vary in their degree and style of focalization, all of which contribute to a multi-valenced experience of Middle-earth. *The Lord of the Rings* is neither flat nor straightforward but contains complexity and deeper meaning in the very way it is told. We hear from many voices — often the voices we least expect to be meaningful offer a crucial perspective. Our journeys in real life are no different. There is a tremendous variety of perspectives to be learned from the people we walk with, but we must choose to ask them what and how they see.

Detours

Not only are the character perspectives complex and enriching, but also the roads these characters travel on are winding and unexpected. As we experience the various wonders and spectacles of Middle-earth with these close-up perspectives, we see that the path to defeating Sauron is anything but direct. Detour after detour interrupts the heroes as they strive to further their purpose.

These interruptions can be ridiculous: for instance, getting eaten by a tree in the Old Forest or having to sit and eat on the sidelines of a battle (*LotR* I.6.117–18; III.3.457–58). They can also be devastating, like Gandalf confronting the Balrog in Moria or Sam chasing after a paralyzed Frodo being carried away by Orcs (*LotR* II.5.331–32; IV.10.735–36). Or they can be extremely pleasant, such as dining with Goldberry and Tom Bombadil or meeting Faramir on the outskirts of Mordor (*LotR* I.7.124; IV.5.680–82). No matter the outcome, the journey through Middle-earth is riddled with detours. Each detour is an additional thread in the overall fabric of the narrative.

Tolkien's story is distinctive in its complex number of narrative threads, many of which are happening simultaneously in time, though they are relayed to the reader in different parts of the book. Sometimes these threads are separated by whole books, leaving the reader uncertain of how other characters are faring for chapters at a time; this is especially the case with Frodo and Sam's journey into Mordor being separate for long periods of time from the rest of the Fellowship's activity. This makes the return to these threads all the more thrilling, allowing us to fill in gaps slowly, experiencing something of the way the characters are also left in uncertainty. C. S. Lewis writes that narratives possessing this simultaneity cause the reader to "lose the feeling that the stories were arbitrarily made up" by the author ("Edmund Spenser, 1552–99" 135). It creates a feeling of reality within the story. There seems to be far more going on behind the scenes that the narrator might be aware of but is not telling us. These background plotlines are essential to the believability and consistency of the story and the world of Middle-earth.

The role of detours comes out clearly in the breaking up of the Fellowship. This event serves as a focal point from which many narrative threads branch out. After all of the respective groups scatter in different directions, the narrative first picks up with Aragorn chasing Frodo. He then rejoins Gimli and Legolas, and together they tend to Boromir's slain body before hunting the orcs that took Merry and Pippin. Second, the reader sees Merry and Pippin carried by the orcs, the orcs themselves serving as a third thread that crosses over the central narrative, though they actually represent three different groups: the Uruk-hai of Saruman, the orcs of Mordor, and the orcs in pursuit of the Fellowship all the way from Moria.[11] Fourth, Sam and Frodo depart east into the Emyn Muil, an event that is not relayed until the beginning of Book IV.

---

[11] The variety of orc parties is discovered later when Pippin overhears the leaders talking (*LotR* III.3.446).

There are several background paths the reader does not see that are nonetheless important to these events. The various orc parties demonstrate that Saruman is involved from afar and that the repercussions of events in Moria continue to impact the Quest. Éomer is setting out to attack the orcs shortly after these events (*LotR* App.B.1092). This is revealed to the reader only in retrospect when Aragorn and Éomer meet, but it also implicates the involvement of Théoden and Wormtongue, whom the reader has not yet met. Gandalf is also active once again in the background. The Great Eagle, Gwaihir, carried him to Lórien a few days earlier, so Gandalf may perhaps still be there when he battles with Sauron's will on Amon Hen, as described from Frodo's inner perspective (*LotR* III.5.499).[12] All of this demonstrates an intricate web of events, revealing a world that is bustling both inside and outside of the reader's view. These intersections give an impression that there is more happening in the world than the reader experiences at any given moment.

This interweaving of many paths that intersect is a narrative technique called "interlace."[13] Interlace is typically associated with medieval romances and Anglo-Saxon poetry.[14] Several Tolkien scholars, including Richard C. West, Tom Shippey, Mary R. Bowman, and Stephen Yandell, explore various examples of interlace in *The Lord of the Rings*. The interlacing of the narrative creates a great deal of variation in how much the reader is made aware of and when. Events unfold with a subtle yet rhythmic alternation between things hidden and things revealed. The primary effect of this variation is a sense of intrigue — not only curiosity or suspense but also the eager anticipation of how and when the characters make discoveries. Tom Shippey argues that the primary effect of the expansive narrative form of interlace is the dramatic irony emerging from "the frequent gaps between what the characters realize and what the reader realizes" (*Author* 107). He highlights moments like when Denethor reveals that

---

[12] Although it is never explicit in the passage that this is Gandalf's doing, it becomes clear based on the timeline in Appendix B and through Gandalf's mention of struggling with Sauron in his conversation with Aragorn, Legolas, and Gimli (*LotR* App B.1092; II.5.499).

[13] A useful analysis of this technique in Tolkien's work appears in Richard C. West's "The Interlace Structure of *The Lord of the Rings*."

[14] For more information on this form's medieval origins, see John Leyerle, "The Interlace Structure of *Beowulf*."

he saw the ships of the corsairs, which leads him to despair. The reader knows by this point in the story that the ships contain reinforcements for Gondor, not Mordor.

An example of this is when Aragorn, Legolas, and Gimli reach Fangorn Forest and stand precisely where Merry and Pippin met Treebeard in the previous chapter (*LotR* III.5.491; III.4.462–63). The return to familiar terrain creates a sense of proximity for the reader — the three pursuers seem close to understanding what happened, yet do not know all the reader knows. The intrigue in this is an anticipation that they will soon find evidence leading them further into the forest. Legolas feels a hint in the stirring of the trees of Fangorn, but only the reader can know it is from the Ents, who are on the verge of marching on Isengard (*LotR* III.5.491). This creates further intrigue, for these three of the Fellowship remain under the impression that Merry and Pippin are helpless and in need of rescue, while the reader knows they are actually taking part in the rousing and eventual march of the Ents. This anticipation is heightened by the fact that they do not continue searching but are diverted by the return of Gandalf.

The complexity of the interlace form is important for giving *The Lord of the Rings* a sense of believability and could even be said to make it a work of realism.[15] Tom Shippey describes the main effect of this technique as not only suspense or surprise but also "a profound sense of reality, of that being *the way things are*" (*Author* 107). Despite the fact that Middle-earth is a world with many fantastic creatures and happenings, those who look closer and study Tolkien's work often discover a great deal of realism. There are whole passages where characters walk, stop, walk, stop, talk, eat, and walk some more. This can feel tedious to even the most loyal reader, but it is a crucial aspect of what makes Tolkien's story compelling. Detours, the boring and the thrilling alike, are an integral part of the journey.

This sense of realism is organic since it reflects the way Tolkien experienced writing the story. He describes the process as the discovery of a world more than the creation of it. Tolkien writes in a letter to W. H. Auden that, in the process of writing, he "met a lot of things on the way" that surprised him (*Letters* 116). He then lists a

---

[15] Christine Brooke-Rose explores whether or not *The Lord of the Rings* is a work of "realism" in the context of literary analysis in "The Evil Ring: Realism and the Marvelous."

long series of events and characters that arose unlooked for during writing but ended up being fundamental to the narrative. Tolkien did not arbitrarily construct plot points or characters for the sake of convenience. He allowed ideas to emerge that felt true to the narrative, though at times he could make little sense of them himself.[16]

To claim that *The Lord of the Rings* is a work of realism is to see that there is something in the technique of interlacing detours that is reflective of our own world. Separate events occur simultaneously, and the depth of their effects on each other is often hidden. This seems a simple truth to say about our own world, but we often operate ignorant of it in our daily lives, assuming we are well-informed of the chain of events leading to our particular situation. Tolkien's narrative demonstrates that detours readily become integral parts of the journey, contributing to the whole rather than being negligible side-quests.

Discoveries

Every journey provides the opportunity for discovery — even if the route, the destination, and the companions are the same as previous trips, there will always be new circumstances to every venture. In addition to learning from focalized perspectives and interlacing detours, we can learn a great deal from the discoveries we make about the new lands, sights, and people encountered on a journey. So much of the world is unseen to us, so the potential is endless for gaining new understanding from it. In the same way that perspectives and detours can surprise us with deeper meaning, the very world itself possesses meaningful things to reveal. The hobbits discover a tremendous number of things by journeying through Middle-earth. Often, these discoveries are not factual but mysterious. The characters learn about the deeper nature of things, finding half-spoken secrets that are stirring and life-changing but cannot be articulated in words. During their Quest, the Fellowship encounters the depth and subtlety of Middle-earth.

The character of Aragorn demonstrates this feature of the narrative well. Different characters at different times gain an ever-deeper understanding of who he is. Their discoveries are often articulated less as gaining knowledge about him and more like a religious revelation.

---

[16] This long list includes items as significant as the character of Faramir, the reason Gandalf could not meet the hobbits in Bree, and the entire forest of Lothlórien (*Letters* 216–17).

The first of these revelations is when the hobbits see Aragorn seem to suddenly grow taller and more authoritative in their small room at the Prancing Pony (*LotR* I.10.171). A further revelation occurs when Frodo comes across a deeply introspective Aragorn in Lothlórien. He seems a prince dressed in white, beholding the memory of what once was there, expressing his desire to remain there forever (*LotR* II.6.352). Seeing Aragorn like this suggests something secret about him. He has been here many times before, but we, like the hobbits, do not know about these other moments in Aragorn's life, seeing only a hint of the greater purposes of his life.

The hobbits see glimpses of Aragorn's deeper identity in his knowledge of lore and shrewdness on the journey, but it is not until entering Gondor on the Great River that they encounter him in his own land. In the shadow of the sentinels Isildur and Anárion, giant stone statues that mark the entrance to the land of Gondor, Frodo is astounded when he turns and beholds a change in Aragorn. Looking at the sentinels, Aragorn has a brightness in his eyes as he recites his full name: "Elessar, the Elfstone son of Arathorn of the House of Valandil Isildur's son, heir of Elendil" (*LotR* II.9.393).[17] He proclaims his lineage, a descendent of the great kings of old depicted in the stone statues. Based on the way Frodo describes him, Aragorn suddenly possesses the splendor of the statues, no longer the foul-looking Ranger of the Prancing Pony.

Revelations of Aragorn's true nature occur again when interacting with the Riders of Rohan. Aragorn declares his full heritage, amazing Legolas, Gimli, and the men of Rohan with his ferocity. Éomer is bewildered at how strange the world is becoming, ancient legends emerging seemingly from nowhere (*LotR* III.2.434–35).[18] The reader, alongside the hobbits, discovers more and more that Aragorn's lineage is the stuff of legend. His decisions to guide the hobbits from Bree and join the ragtag Fellowship challenge expectations of how great,

---

[17] For additional insight into the importance of names in Middle-earth, see the section "Familial Connections" in Ch. 3, "Enchantment in Middle-earth" in Ch. 8, and "Reflecting on Trees" in Zeimis's discussion of Old Entish in Ch. 9.

[18] Other examples of Aragorn's increasingly significant role include Éowyn seeing him as an ancient, hidden power, Legolas's description of him riding before the armies of the dead with such power and authority that he seemed to possess the Ring, and the description of him finally crowned king of Gondor (*LotR* III.6.515; V.9.876; VI.5.968).

mythical heroes ought to behave. Aragorn's repeated unveilings are more potent because his typical appearance in the story is gruff and commonplace. His true nature is obscured and secretive, but these successive revelations of his nature emphasize his deeper role and purpose in the narrative.

Although it is not expanded upon explicitly, part of the significance of Aragorn's role in Middle-earth arises from the deeper mythology that undergirds the narrative. Middle-earth's history is vast and intricate. It demonstrates the narrative technique that Tolkien is perhaps best known for: world-building.[19] Tolkien's world is immense. Inklings scholar Clyde S. Kilby notes that *The Lord of the Rings* contains over 600 references to the history of Middle-earth, demonstrating its essential role (Kilby 45). This body of background history can be referred to as Tolkien's personal mythology,[20] while the expansive body of manuscripts and writings expounding upon this history is referred to as the legendarium.[21]

Tolkien began developing this mythology as early as 1914, many years before he conceived of *The Hobbit* or *The Lord of the Rings* (*Letters* 221). Mythology was of great importance to Tolkien. In a letter to publisher Milton Waldman, he explains his longtime passion for myth and his inability to find enough of it to satisfy him (*Letters* 144). In his essay "On Fairy-stories" Tolkien writes that "history often resembles 'Myth,' because they are both made of the same stuff" (FS 30). This is

---

[19] Some Tolkien scholars distinguish between world-building and Tolkien's own word for the technique, "sub-creation," from his essay "On Fairy-stories." For the present purposes, the term world-building is more appropriate since it remains in common usage both in Tolkien studies and for popular audiences. For technical purposes, the distinction is useful. For an excellent collection of essays on this technique, see *Sub-creating Arda*, edited by Dimitra Fimi and Thomas Honegger. David Bratman also emphasizes the value of this distinction between world-building and sub-creation in his review of *Sub-creating Arda* in the journal *Tolkien Studies*.

[20] Due to the tremendous work of Tolkien's son Christopher Tolkien, much of this background history is available in published volumes. The best starting point is *The Silmarillion*, the history of Middle-earth that Tolkien actively worked on and desperately wanted to get published. Originally, Tolkien believed a reader of *The Lord of the Rings* would be lost without having read *The Silmarillion* and almost switched publishers in order to get it published in one volume with *The Lord of the Rings* (S x).

[21] I owe to David Bratman the more specific definition of "legendarium" in Tolkien scholarship.

why the history and mythology of Middle-earth are indistinguishable. The wider histories of Middle-earth serve as an undergirding force in the narrative of *The Lord of the Rings*. Most of the discoveries we or the characters experience along the way possess a rich allure due to their vague but solid connection to the history behind the narrative. Sometimes the narrator does this by blatant explanation, sometimes by suggestion, and sometimes by obscuring even further. These connections are like secrets that skirt around the edges of the story, impacting its meaning and deepening its significance.

The deeper world of Middle-earth allows us to deepen our understanding of Aragorn even further. One example of this is the way his relationship with Arwen in many ways parallels the legend of Beren and Lúthien. A fascinating legend in its fullness, the core of the story is that Beren, a man, and Lúthien, an elf, fall in love with each other, and Lúthien decides to give up her immortality for Beren in the same way Arwen does for Aragorn (*S* 162–87).[22] Aragorn is a lore-master as well as a figure in the lore, a manifestation of history active and moving in the present of *The Lord of the Rings*.[23] Understanding the mythology accentuates the significance of the hobbits' fortune in meeting him in Bree, his return to the throne of Gondor, and his marriage to Arwen.

Tolkien's mastery of storytelling is displayed by the fact that his reader does not *need* to know the mythology to benefit from its influence. The characters and readers alike discover many things throughout the narrative. There is a mystical, or even a spiritual, element to the way discoveries occur in *The Lord of the Rings*. Philosopher Hannah

---

[22] The story of Beren and Lúthien is one of the oldest legends in Tolkien's mythology (*LotR* App. A.I.3.1057–63).

[23] "Lore-master" is used throughout the narrative to describe characters like Aragorn, Gandalf, Denethor, and Saruman. Tolkien defines lore in a letter to Milton Waldman as "the preservation in reverent memory of all tradition concerning the good, wise, and beautiful" (*S* xx). The role of lore-master in Middle-earth indicates being learned in its deeper realities. The lore-master's power resides in their knowledge of legend and myth rather than mere martial or physical prowess, though many of the lore-masters are formidable in battle as well. The association of lore to power and leadership is worth further exploration, especially in regard to Frodo's suggestion that Sam must take on the role of Hobbit lore-master, collecting and remembering all the legends and histories so that they remain revered and instructive (*LotR* VI.9.1029). Previously, Gandalf was the only one of the Wise who chose to study Hobbit-lore (*LotR* I.2.48). Frodo's initiation of Sam into the role of lore-master suggests the growing place of Hobbits in the wider world beyond their fame for overthrowing Sauron.

Arendt's words capture it well. Arendt claims that, though a life of constant display and publicity is hyper-visible, it is shallow and "loses the quality of rising into sight from some darker ground which must remain hidden if it is not to lose its depth in a very real, non-subjective sense" (71). There is something in a quest that remains ineffable. The aspects of our journeys that evade explanation are often the deepest and most formative. This ineffability can arise out of the depths of sorrow and loss as well as the utmost delight and bliss. The inability to explain these experiences does not diminish their impact on our lives but actually signals a more serious, foundational influence.

Vitality
One of the most captivating parts of Tolkien's Middle-earth that *The Lord of the Rings* allows us to experience first-hand is the vitality of the land itself. Throughout the story, the characters and readers discover that Middle-earth's landscape is subtly but definitely alive.[24] One of the most obvious examples of this is the very existence of Ents, but there are many other examples varying widely in tone.[25] The four hobbits feel the Old Forest clearly exert a will of threat and malice (*LotR* I.6.112), Legolas hears the stones of Hollin speak out their sorrow (*LotR* II.3.283), and Gimli shows Frodo the power of the Mirrormere as it slowly reveals a sky of stars in full daylight (*LotR* II.6.334). This vitality of place grows scarcer in the realm of Men, according well with their history of not being as in touch with the divinities of Middle-earth.[26] This explains the fear that Men have of Lothlórien,

---

[24] For a detailed account of environmental interpretations of *The Lord of the Rings*, see Matthew T. Dickerson and Jonathan Evans, *Ents, Elves, and Eriador: The Environmental Vision of J. R. R. Tolkien*.

[25] For an exploration of the Ents and their significance in Middle-earth, see Zeimis's section "Reflecting on Trees" in Ch. 9.

[26] Hobbits and Men are most frequently astonished by the truth of legends, likely due to their shorter lifespans and seeming disconnect from the magic of Middle-earth. This disconnection is demonstrated in *The Silmarillion*'s account of Men's origin story "Of Men." It is said that the deities of Middle-earth, the Valar, sent messages of counsel through the streams and the rivers, but humans "have not skill in such matters," especially before they interacted with the Elves. So, in looking in the waters, "their hearts were stirred, but they understood not the messages" (*S* 103–04). Aragorn, as a descendent of the race of men who mingled with the Elves, is in touch with such things, as are Legolas and Gimli in their own ways. As Britta E. Bunnel pointed out to me, legends are indistinguishable from history for the immortal Elves, hence the presence of lore-masters rather than

which serves as a primary example of a living landscape. Everything in Lothlórien feels alive with vibrancy. A single *mallorn* seed and a bit of soil are potent enough to reforest all of the Shire, making it more beautiful than it was before (*LotR* VI.9.1022–23).

Desecrated landscapes also possess this vitality, as Frodo and Sam experience on the outskirts of Mordor. The menace is similar to the impression the Fellowship gets of Caradhras (*LotR* II.3.289). In the Dead Marshes, the narrator describes the reeds as hissing like evil creatures (*LotR* IV.2.625). Shortly after this, Frodo is horrified by the corruption of the lands outside of Mordor, where the landscape is described as choking, gasping, feeding on rottenness, and crawling with mud (*LotR* IV.2.631). The very air and light of this place feel corrupted, like an ally of the Enemy against the hobbits. When Frodo's laughter echoes about the stairs of Cirith Ungol, Sam sees the stone cliffs around him lean in, as though threatened by the presence of such joy in their land of woe (*LotR* IV.8.712). There is a deep resonance of meaning in the very landscape of Middle-earth. This vitality provides a vibrancy that is enticing and provocative. Much more is in store for the hobbits than they ever imagined before they set out.

It is helpful to think of this literary device less as personification, which suggests creative interpretation of a subject toward an object, and more as landscape vocalization. The narrator gives voice to the landscape, meaning it has a life of its own. However, this voice is only communicated to the reader through particular characters' perspectives, such as Legolas in Hollin or Sam in Mordor.[27] This indicates that the technique is closely tied to focalization, yet remains distinct.

---

historians. The Men of Rohan and Gondor do not have an intuitive sense of the divine power and life existing in Middle-earth. This suggests that the vitality of the land very much exists, even if an entire race is unable to notice it. Skepticism does not indicate nonexistence, nor does it mean the ignorant party is unaffected by the unseen plane.

[27] A modern reader might want to suggest that this signifies room for the interpretation that the landscape is not *actually* alive, but that the characters in the story are experiencing it in this way, i.e., it is merely the characters' subjective experience of Middle-earth. Within the narrative, however, characters such as Treebeard and Tom Bombadil attest to the fact that the landscape is very much alive. The vitality of the landscape always being focalized through particular characters does not indicate the potential falsity of the experience as much as it suggests the necessity of attending to the world. In the context of Tolkien's world, the life of the landscape is not a matter of subjective interpretation. Rather, it is a matter of awareness.

This landscape vocalization creates a vitality of place in Tolkien's world. It is a simple but essential piece of *The Lord of the Rings* that the very land, soil, and trees of Middle-earth are not merely lifeless material. They are certainly physical, but their physicality does not exclude them from possessing an ability to resonate more deeply with animation, with meaning, and with influence. Steve Walker writes about the power of Tolkien's sense of place in *The Power of Tolkien's Prose*. Walker claims that "everything can feel. Anything may move. Will is everywhere. Middle-earth insists in its very setting that everything, however insensate or trivial it may seem to be, matters" (47). The feeling of vitality in the story is one of the effects of the world-building technique.

The world is vital. We as the readers alongside the characters get to see the often bewildering exercises of this vitality. Vitality of place also contributes to the overall theme of journeys: paying attention to the perspectives, detours, and discoveries along the way gives the journey a sense of deeper life, a vibrancy that can be dangerous and forbidding, but also expressive and inviting.

Tolkien's Quest

Somewhere around 1:00 a.m., still within twenty miles of their home, Sam, Frodo, and Pippin sleep cozily beneath some fir trees. The campfire slowly calms from a busy blaze to a dull wavering. The three hobbits rest snugly in the night, their minds at ease. They have been warned of shadows and darkness but have yet to encounter such things for themselves, so they can still rest easy. How could they realize that back in Hobbiton a terrifying shadow from the depths of history hunts for them? Why should they fear such a thing? They are still in the Shire, after all, and all is familiar.

The only intruders on this night are the native forest animals, including a fox. This fox, we are told, is quite baffled at the spectacle before him: hobbits traveling away from the Shire, in the dark, even sleeping outside! Though the fox is aware of many strange happenings of late, this seems most perplexing of all: three hobbits sleeping outside in the discomfort of the woods! The narrator then points out that the fox "was quite right, but he never found out any more about it" (*LotR* I.3.72).

I return to my question from the beginning: why would Tolkien decide to include this description of a solitary fox? An initial thought might be that it is a leftover from an earlier draft when Tolkien still viewed this book as a children's story, a proper sequel to *The Hobbit*. However, Tolkien was meticulous in his revisions, neglecting no details and demanding absolute consistency. Over nearly two decades of writing and rewriting, this description of a fox's thoughts remains.

Analyzing through the lens of the narrative techniques discussed, we gain some traction in understanding this passage. All four of the narrative techniques suggest that this moment fits well, not only as a narrative device but with the overall themes and preoccupations of the story. First, the reader is getting a close-up, intimate perspective of the fox, just as the narrator focalizes the narrative through other specific characters. The general description crystalizes for a couple of sentences into an intimate and meaningful new perspective. Second, this fox crosses the path of the main plotline for one short page, but his detour to investigate these hobbits adds to the feeling of activity. The world of Middle-earth is moving and active beyond the main events the reader sees. So, in a small way, this description of the fox adds to the realism and believability of the world, even as it is also a quiet element of fantasy.

Third, there is more to be discovered about animals in Middle-earth than we might expect. There is precedent in the legendarium for animals having something to say, such as the great dog Huan in the story of Beren and Lúthien who is said to have spoken only three times in his life (*S* 173). Later, the reader will encounter the Great Eagles, who are capable of speech, and rumors of the ancestral horse of Eorl that could speak the language of Men (*LotR* III.2.435). A fox's thoughts on the hobbits give just a hint of this feature of Middle-earth. Fourth, the entrance of this fox is like a shocking breath of life and vitality. Suddenly, the nature of Middle-earth is more alive and awake than the reader has yet experienced. The fox account primes the reader to experience meaningful aspects of the narrative from all sorts of sources, including the landscape, or a mere fox.

While this description of the fox's perspective is not necessary to the Quest, this does not mean it is devoid of value. Our expectations of what is important often blind us from seeing the reality of the world around us. Looking deeper at *The Lord of the Rings* reminds us that reality is neither simple nor easily discernible. We think we know the people around us, we assume we know the direction that we ought to walk, we fool ourselves into believing we have discovered all that we need to know, and we fall into believing the natural world is nothing but dead matter.[28]

Allowing these assumptions to remain inhibits our ability to pay attention to what really matters, especially when it is needed most. This cultivates a lifestyle of ignorance toward the people walking beside us, abhorrence of any bump or detour, distraction from the discoveries yet in store, and negligence of the quiet but powerful vitality permeating the world. Tolkien's narrative leads us to expect significance from unlikely places and lessons from unlikely sources. The journey through Middle-earth is worth the time — and, as the next chapters elaborate, it is worth journeying back again and again. The narrative techniques discussed here are but one attempt to show why Tolkien's story grows richer with every reading. *The Lord of the Rings* reminds us to see in our own world how many sources of wonder, conviction, and wisdom exist beyond the small door of our own Bag End.

---

[28] This resonates with Harbman's focus in Ch. 8 on enchantment and disenchantment, especially the discussion of Tolkien's poem "Mythopoeia" in the section "Tolkien's Worldview."

Chapter 2

Unexpected Worth
Jordan F. Mar

During Sam and Frodo's ascent of Mount Doom, Sam makes the difficult choice to discard the items in his pack. This includes a set of pans that he has carried with him throughout the journey. In an effort to alleviate the physical difficulties of their climb, Sam reluctantly throws his cooking gear and "precious pans" into a mountain fissure (*LotR* VI.3.938).[29] Tears come to his eyes, and the clanging of Sam's pans is compared to a somber "death-knell to his heart" (*LotR* VI.3.938). Tolkien surprises readers with Sam's deep emotion regarding these materials. In the middle of the Quest to destroy the Ring, Tolkien pauses the storyline to focus on cooking gear. Certainly, pans are not usually included in stories of heroic adventures, but they are in this one.[30]

Sam's cooking materials appear to be nothing exceptional or spectacular. He may have been emotionally attached to these pans simply due to the fact they had traveled across Middle-earth just as far as he had (*LotR* VI.3.397). Beyond that, these cooking supplies could have brought him the comfort of knowing that he could sustain himself and Frodo for the rest of the journey. Maybe they serve as a reminder of the small comforts from home that remained with them throughout the Quest. And perhaps most importantly, these treasured tools are necessary for the skill and talent of cooking that Sam regards

---

[29] The use of the adjective "precious" is reminiscent of the description attached primarily to the One Ring. It is worth noting that Sam's pans, like the Ring, are viewed as "precious" in the eyes of the owners. Tolkien did not make a direct comment on the use of the word "precious" in this particular scene, but this description of Sam's pans greatly emphasizes that these pans have significant value for Sam.

[30] In Ch. 1, Kirkendall highlights how Tolkien employs the technique of focalization, as seen in this passage, to help create a more nuanced experience of the characters.

as his "chief treasure" (*LotR* II.3.280; IV.4.653).[31] Regardless of Sam's various reasons for treasuring the pans, it is clear that they matter, and this is especially evident when Sam must continue on without them.

Ordinary Objects
Sam's esteem for ordinary objects is echoed in Tolkien's *Hobbit*, a prequel to *The Lord of the Rings*, when Thorin Oakenshield says to Bilbo: "If more of us valued food and cheer and song above hoarded gold, it would be a merrier world" (*H* 348). Ordinary pleasures and everyday objects ought to be deeply cherished and, at times, more treasured than gold, even if outside appearances are lackluster. *The Lord of the Rings* and the world of Middle-earth exemplify this very concept. The elevation of ordinary objects is a lens that Tolkien invites his readers to look through as they journey through Middle-earth.

Tolkien's experience in World War I may have influenced his emphasis on unassuming objects. In transit to a new army division, Tolkien stopped in Calais, France, at the base camp called Étaples. In the confusion of war, all of his supplies were misplaced in the transition (Garth 143–44). He was without his boots, bedding, and other necessities. This was a great loss for a soldier who was far from home in bitterly cold quarters with no bedding and greatly limited in opportunity to buy new equipment. These objects were so important that Tolkien had no choice but to beg and borrow from other soldiers in order to replace the lost items. All of these objects were absolutely ordinary, so it is tempting to dismiss their importance. But, similar to the loss of Sam's pans, the loss of Tolkien's seemingly commonplace supplies reminds readers that such simple objects can make a profound difference.

Another example of the emphasis on ordinary objects is the use of kingsfoil in the House of Healing in Gondor. After the battle on the fields of Pelennor, Aragorn visits Faramir, Éowyn, and Merry, who were severely injured in battle. In an attempt to heal them, Aragorn requests a plant called kingsfoil. Even after his request, the Gondor citizens dismiss the importance of kingsfoil as not having "any great virtue" and degrade its value to that of a common "weed" (*LotR* V.8.864–65). Kingsfoil, according to the herb-master, is normally used for air freshener or a quick remedy for headaches. But that is not its

---

[31] This observation is credited to David Bratman.

only use. In the pages that follow, kingsfoil is used to waken and begin the healing process for Faramir, Éowyn, and Merry after their encounter with the Nazgûl's Black Breath. This is another instance in which Tolkien focuses on the seemingly ordinary object. In this case, that object becomes integral to the story. It might have been much simpler for Tolkien to skip these sections entirely or shorten these events to a few sentences. Yet, he uses several pages of the story to explain the hidden value of this plant.

Some may read *The Lord of the Rings* with slight amusement or even annoyance because of the detours Tolkien takes to describe such small everyday objects. But a closer look at Middle-earth suggests that Tolkien uses these detailed accounts as a reminder that ordinary things are to be cherished and regarded as important. Pans are not *just* pans. A healing plant is not *just* a useless weed. And a ring is not *just* jewelry. Overlooked objects certainly have the potential to change the course of everyday life and even whole worlds.

Ordinary Background
Like simple objects, the inhabitants of Middle-earth may also have more worth than what is initially perceived. Hobbits are an example of a race that is more than what is seen at first glance. They are described as "unobtrusive" beings who enjoy the simple things in life, such as a well-ordered home, farming, abundant food, and family (*LotR* Prologue.I.1). But these individuals deserve a closer look if one is to gain a richer understanding of Tolkien's Middle-earth. Tolkien's descriptive history of Hobbits in the prologue highlights just how ordinary they are. Many find it easy to skim through the prologue while simultaneously wondering why Tolkien inserted such a long introduction about the somewhat bland Hobbit life. In fact, some audiobook recordings of *The Lord of the Rings* skip the prologue altogether and insert it at the end, as if it were some sort of appendix. But when readers skip the prologue, they miss the crucial first sentence: "This book is largely concerned with Hobbits" (*LotR* Prologue.I.1). This sentence and the rest of the prologue are foundational to the story.

Gaining a fuller understanding of the Shire and Hobbit life achieves two purposes. First, it allows readers to recognize the motivations of the hobbits, specifically Frodo. When Gandalf initially presents the Quest, Frodo's first instinct is to save the home that he loves (*LotR* I.2.62). Tolkien scholar Stratford Caldecott points out that "it is our knowledge of a light and a beauty worth defending that inspires heroism — even the heroism of Hobbits, who are inspired to risk their lives by their love of the homely beauty of the Shire" ("Horns" 44–45). The simple life led by the Hobbits is both valuable and worth defending. There are multiple instances in their adventures when the journeying hobbits long for the simple pleasures of home — whether that be a stout beer, a good smoke of quality pipe-weed, or just some plain taters. It is their love for home that inspires them to face the dangers of the outside world.

Secondly and perhaps more importantly, this emphasis on simple Shire life causes the reader to better relate to the hobbits (Flieger, "Frodo and Aragorn" 124). Clyde B. Northrup observes that "Hobbits live in an agrarian society, where peace, quiet and frequent meals are the rule. There is little about them that makes them different from humans" (820). Tolkien's shaping of Shire life allows many readers to connect easily with the Hobbits and gain practical insights from the connection.

Furthermore, it is easy to discount the difference that Hobbits make in Middle-earth because they have such an ordinary background. This is seen when Frodo thinks to himself at the gates of Mordor: "and here he was a little halfling from the Shire, a simple hobbit of the quiet countryside, expected to find a way where the great ones could not go, or dared not go" (*LotR* IV.3.644). Even though Hobbits do have a history, the background of the Hobbit-folk is simply not the same as the deep lore of Dwarves, Elves, or Men. They are simple, mundane countryfolk. In this moment, Frodo realizes that the "great ones" such as Aragorn or Gandalf had never traveled through Mordor. Most would ask the same question that Frodo does: how could a simple hobbit accomplish something that people with such marvelous backgrounds had never even attempted? Surely, someone else with more importance, skill, and power should have attempted this journey.

Ordinary Hero
Frodo believes that heroes such as Aragorn or Gandalf are more suited to bear the Ring to Mordor than he is. Like Frodo, readers would expect characters such as these to traverse the perils of Mordor and save Middle-earth. There are certain qualities about characters like Aragorn and Gandalf generally associated with a typical hero (Flieger, "Frodo and Aragorn" 124). In Aragorn, Tolkien creates the archetypal "romantic hero" (Frye 33–35). He is admired, wields a legendary

sword, fights off the enemy, protects the people, has supernatural gifts of healing, marries his beloved Arwen, and is finally crowned king. Certainly, Aragorn could have fulfilled the role of the hero.

However, that is not Tolkien's story. Heroes like Aragorn and Gandalf certainly play powerful roles individually in the effort to save Middle-earth, and this chapter does not seek to downplay this heroism.[32] These characters are simply not the focus of the narrative. Rather, it is the humble hobbit who saves Middle-earth. For Tolkien, the story was meant to "be 'hobbito-centric,' that is, primarily a study of the ennoblement (or sanctification) of the humble" (*Letters* 232). Readers have a completely different reading experience as they follow the adventures of each hobbit — one that may not have even existed if the story had been focused on other types of heroes.

This type of humble hero is the one to ultimately bring about the success of the mission. According to Shippey, Frodo Baggins is a "low mimetic" hero (*Author* 316). He comes from a plain upbringing, is underqualified, makes plenty of mistakes, and does not believe in his own abilities. However, it is this inadequacy that Tolkien brings into the spotlight. *The Lord of the Rings* reminds readers that those who "move the wheels of the world" (*LotR* II.2.269) are the ordinary and seemingly insignificant (Chance, "Tolkien's Epic" 154). Even though Frodo is unable to relinquish the Ring at the final moment, his journey leading up to Mount Doom must not be undervalued. Frodo persists despite tremendous challenges and plays an indispensable role in saving the day.

One can focus so much on Frodo as the main Ring-bearer that the impact of faithful Sam Gamgee can be overlooked. Sam exemplifies the most simple and ordinary of Hobbits. He is a gardener and has no outstanding physical skill. Even his own friends believe that he is incapable of assisting Frodo without sabotaging the entire mission (*LotR* I.5.104). In spite of Sam's obvious weaknesses, Tolkien calls him

---

[32] Scholars have continued to delve into the complexity of Tolkien's heroic characters. There are those that Tolkien uses to represent heroes of the classic romance epic tales such as Aragorn, but characters such as Frodo, Sam, Merry, and Pippin also represent the heroes of classic fairy-stories. The complexity of Tolkien's narrative acknowledges the intertwining of the different classifications of hero. This collaboration is necessary for the success of the mission. However, in personal letters written by Tolkien, it is clear that while teamwork is part of the narrative, the hobbit-folk are the focus of the story. See Thomas Honegger, "Splintered Heroes."

the "most heroic character" (*Letters* 244). After all, Sam battles both Gollum and Shelob (*LotR* IV.9.725–26; IV.10.728–30). Sam takes on the burden of the Ring when he believes Frodo to be dead (*LotR* IV.10.733). Sam loses sleep to protect his master from potential dangers (*LotR* VI.2.929). Sam sacrifices his own shares of food to nourish Frodo (*LotR* VI.2.928–29). Sam frees Frodo from the orcs by storming the Tower of Cirith Ungol alone (*LotR* VI.1.903–10). Sam physically carries Frodo up Mount Doom (*LotR* VI.3.938–44). And most shockingly, this mere gardener from the Shire does not succumb to the temptation of the Ring (*LotR* VI.1.900–01; Chance, "Tolkien's Epic" 180).

It is ultimately Sam's courage and stubborn hope that empower Frodo to continue on through Mordor. Sam's acts of bravery transform our expectation of what a hero looks like. Heroes can certainly be found among the strong, but they can also be found in the smallest and humblest of characters like Samwise Gamgee. Steady persistence and simple acts of courage allow ordinary hobbits to go and do what the greats would not dare.

Tolkien's emphasis on the actions of Sam and Frodo gives readers a richer and more diverse understanding of what a hero can look like. His experiences during WWI shed light on what he thought of these smaller but crucial acts of heroism. Humphrey Carpenter notes that Tolkien himself was deeply moved by the "indomitable courage of quite small people against impossible odds" shown by soldiers in the trenches (180). John Garth emphasizes that "Tolkien's protagonists are heroes not because of their successes, which are often limited, but because of their courage and tenacity in trying" (303). This type of "indomitable courage" is found in stepping onto the battlefield to face unknowable terrors and potential death. It is the ordinary courage found by taking one step at a time up Mount Doom with only the smallest amount of hope for success as motivation. Ordinary courage protected the world that Tolkien lived in and is echoed in those who save Middle-earth.

Ordinary Battles
After their journey across Middle-earth, the four hobbits find themselves back in the Shire. Before departing from the four friends, Gandalf says, "You must settle [the Shire's] affairs yourselves; that is what you have been trained for" (*LotR* VI.7.996). Gandalf sends them home with full knowledge that their adventures in the outside world truly prepared them to encounter the trouble in the Shire (Dickerson 233).

Two examples of this are Merry and Pippin. At the beginning of the Quest, Merry and Pippin are immature and ill-equipped for such a dangerous journey. This is seen in Elrond's firm discouragement of their intention to join Frodo and Sam on the Quest (*LotR* II.3.276). However, both grow immensely as they learn from experiences with other leaders like Aragorn, Gandalf, Denethor, and Théoden.[33] Their process of growth is seen even more when both hobbits blatantly defy the commands given to them, risk punishment from their superiors, and save others from a worse fate.[34] Readers witness Pippin's heroic disobedience of Denethor's commands in an attempt to save the life of Faramir (*LotR* V.4.827). In a similar way, marked growth for Merry also takes place under the authority of Théoden. Merry's resolute courage is seen when he ignores Théoden's order to not participate in the Battle of the Pelennor Fields (*LotR* V.3.804).

Although this is not directly seen in the text, Merry and Pippin most likely learn from the actions of Gandalf, Aragorn, and others who are more experienced. They are influenced by these leaders to actively participate in the fight against Sauron even if that means risking their lives. These acts of defiance have a deep impact because Pippin helps to save Faramir and Merry defies all expectations in his cooperative role in slaying the Lord of the Nazgûl.[35] They are no longer the immature and ill-equipped hobbits that readers meet at the beginning of the adventure.

After these experiences, the hobbits do not come home to the same Shire they left behind. They return to a land infiltrated by

---

[33] Merry and Pippin also grow up physically as a result of the Ent-draught that Treebeard gave them (Langford 5–6).

[34] It is significant that both Pippin and Merry disobey direct orders from Denethor and Théoden after they make binding oaths to serve each of them. However, their conscious disobedience has a profound impact on those around them. This illustrates the challenge of determining whether and when explicit disobedience is called for. Unfortunately, this topic cannot be explored in this chapter with the attention it deserves. Jonathan D. Langford expands upon this in "The Scouring of the Shire as a Hobbit Coming-of-Age" in relation to how Pippin and Merry mature in this area. Readers may explore other events of active disobedience for what could be considered the greater good in the actions of Éowyn disguising herself to fight and Beregond leaving his post to save Faramir. The section "Broadening the Scope" in Ch. 6 explores how mercy and pity influence the way Beregond settles the conflict between disobeying orders and saving Faramir.

[35] Turn to the "Unexpectedly Useful Objects" section in Ch. 7 to see how providence is at work in Merry's heroic actions.

tyranny as Saruman (disguised as Sharkey) corrupts the Shire. After experiencing the weight of evil in the outside world, the hobbits find injustice in the Shire and fight yet another battle. This battle is different in that it is right at home, and the forces of evil also do not look the same. But with a closer inspection, "The Scouring of the Shire" can be seen as a parallel to the battles faced earlier. Instead of facing orcs, the hobbits face Shirriffs. "Sharkey" is the big threat at home rather than Sauron. And they battle face-to-face with ruffians instead of Ringwraiths.[36] Each of the Shire counterparts is smaller and arguably less intimidating than what the hobbits faced prior to their return.

However, due to their confrontation with evil throughout the Quest, Merry and Pippin are more equipped to fight against this injustice. As Gandalf said, the lessons they learned from their journey fully prepare them for the battle in the Shire. Just as they disobeyed orders from Théoden and Denethor, the two hobbits defy the new rulers of the Shire. Additionally, they work to defend others even if that means risking their own safety. Although the occupation of the Shire is on a smaller scale than the War of the Ring, it is worth fighting. Merry and Pippin could have easily dismissed the importance of the Shire battle, as the forces of evil they face at home are diminutive in comparison to what they saw on their Quest. Rather, both hobbits treat this battle with seriousness because the battle of the Shire and the battles fought throughout their journey are fought for the same reason: preservation of simple Shire life.

Ordinary Life

After the battle against the oppressors of the Shire, Tolkien quickly shifts the story back to what ordinary life looks like for the hobbits, whether that is raising a family, cultivating the garden, or fixing houses. Charles Williams, a close friend of Tolkien's, observed that the center of *The Lord of the Rings* "is not in strife and war and heroism (though they are understood and depicted) but in freedom, peace, [and] ordinary life" (*Letters* 105). In reality, everyday life is not made up of war and grand quests. Most of life takes place right at home — in

---

[36] Bernhard Hirsch compares this final portion of Tolkien's narrative to a coda — a musical term used to describe the conclusion of an orchestral piece. Additionally, a coda modifies and reminds the listener of common themes already heard throughout the song. Hirsch concludes that this part of Tolkien's story serves to remind readers of the themes they already encountered (90–94).

the perfectly ordinary. Tolkien emphasizes this ordinary life to remind readers that seemingly small acts like gardening or fixing houses are nothing to be ashamed of, but instead should be celebrated.

This can be seen clearly in the last chapter of the story. Readers may finish the story, close the book, and move on to the next great novel. But this section is where Tolkien delivers his final message.[37] In the last paragraph of the book, Sam returns back to normal life — a warm home, a hot meal, and his family. The final spoken words of the book are: "well, I'm back" (*LotR* VI.9.1031).[38] Tolkien leaves the story open-ended with this final line. This word "back" evokes a feeling of both returning and potential (Caldecott, "Horns" 44). "Back" is an invitation to return to the mundane and effect change through living an ordinary life. Although Middle-earth is safe for now, the life of each character is not over. Life at home is accorded the same worth given to the heroics done in the outside world (Greenwood 193).

The hobbits of the Fellowship undoubtedly change the course of Middle-earth's history, but they also work to move and shape the community to which they return. This involves planting new gardens, as Sam does, or spreading general merriment, as Merry and Pippin do

---

[37] Tolkien wrote several versions of an unpublished epilogue that delves into the future of Samwise Gamgee. This epilogue gives readers a glimpse into Sam's ordinary family life after Frodo's departure to the Otherworld of the Valar. It, too, emphasizes returning to ordinary life. It appears in *Sauron Defeated: The End of the Third Age*, The History of Middle-earth, Volume 9. According to a letter Tolkien wrote in 1954, the epilogue had "been so universally condemned that I shall not insert it. One must stop somewhere" (*Letters* 179). Since that chapter was not included in the original publication, this section focuses on the ending that is generally accessible for the reader.

[38] The format and the final words of *The Lord of the Rings* are a subtle reference to the subtitle of Tolkien's *Hobbit* in that the characters go *There and Back Again* (Hirsch 77–107). In context, these words also allude to Sam returning to his beloved family as promised. In a grander sense, Sam has just seen the departure of Bilbo and Frodo while he is the only Ring-bearer returning back to ordinary life. I am indebted to David Bratman for these observations. Additionally, I would be remiss to not reference Tolkien's experience in WWI as someone who returns home without his beloved friends. For Tolkien, the concept of coming back from the Great War while many companions would never come back should be noted as an influence on these final scenes. It is significant that Sam was able to return home and fully enter into Shire society while Frodo was not able to. This parallels the experience of many men and women after WWI. John Garth's *Tolkien and the Great War: The Threshold of Middle-earth* offers more details regarding Tolkien's deep friendships and his experience as a survivor of WWI.

(*LotR* VI.9.1025).[39] Some would presume that simple domestic life is unimportant, but remaining diligent in ordinary duties can be just as essential as fighting wars.

One character who exemplifies this is Farmer Maggot. At the beginning of their adventures, Frodo, Sam, and Pippin encounter the farmer as they leave the Shire (*LotR* I.4.91–97). He provides them with dinner, transportation, and a basket of delicious mushrooms. The hobbits also learn of his courage in the face of potential danger when he recounts his confrontation with the Black Rider. A closer examination of the text shows that Farmer Maggot is essential to the advancement of the journey (Dickerson and Evans 75–86). Farmer Maggot is the first character to generously show hospitality to the hobbits on their journey. This act of kindness is one of many that alleviate the difficulties of such an arduous Quest. Additionally, Farmer Maggot's defiant refusal to reveal Frodo's location to the Black Rider keeps the hobbits safe, if only for a while. Although this safety is short-lived, it is still crucial to the beginning of their journey.

Farmer Maggot's hospitality and courage truly lay a foundation for the rest of the Quest, but the farmer himself is oblivious to the vital role that he plays. In this scene, he is simply helping the hobbit travelers and living his ordinary life as a farmer. After this brief interaction, Farmer Maggot is mentioned once again when Tom Bombadil says that Farmer Maggot is "of more importance than [the hobbits] had imagined" (*LotR* I.7.132). This humble farmer is someone whom the hobbits had dismissed as unimportant, yet the exact opposite is true. Although Farmer Maggot leads an ordinary life, Tom Bombadil's comment correctly asserts that this simple farmer has a larger role in the story than the hobbits (or readers) may have thought.

Realistically, most people do not embark on grand adventures every day to fight face-to-face with looming evils such as Sauron or the Ring. Life looks much simpler: maintaining the house, going to work,

---

[39] *The Lord of the Rings* scholarship frequently recognizes that Frodo's role as the main Ring-bearer deeply impacts him. His return to the Shire is significantly different from the return that Sam, Merry, and Pippin experience, as seen in the smaller role he plays in the Battle of Bywater when comparing his actions to those of Sam, Merry, and Pippin. Frodo's change is also suggested by his inability to successfully assimilate back into ordinary life as the other hobbits do. More on this can be found in Verlyn Flieger's "Frodo and Aragorn" and Fleming Rutledge's *The Battle for Middle-earth: Tolkien's Divine Design in* The Lord of the Rings.

and taking care of family and friends. *The Lord of the Rings* reminds readers that the truly valuable does not need to be glamorous. A life that is significant and meaningful can be led on the battlefield but also on the doorstep of our own homes. The ordinary and overlooked resonate with ordinary readers when we see them for what they are: extraordinary.

Being able to recognize the extraordinary worth of the ordinary requires a careful examination of every person and object rather than a casual dismissal of what seems unimportant. When Pippin and Gandalf arrive at Minas Tirith, Denethor interrogates Pippin about how Boromir could have possibly been killed while a weak hobbit such as Pippin could have escaped (*LotR* V.1.755). Denethor's attitude toward Pippin is full of "scorn and suspicion" which, according to Jane Chance, points towards Denethor's narrow perception (*LotR* V.1.755). Denethor's limited outlook causes him to "assume that 'small' means helpless and weak and that 'large' means strong and able" (Chance, "Power and the Community" 100–01). He is quick to judge Pippin's abilities by merely glancing at his outer appearance.

The quick dismissal of ordinary Hobbits is also a fault of Sauron and Saruman (Chance, "Power and the Community" 101). These characters do not realize the crucial effects of ordinary heroes who play significant roles in their ultimate downfall. Sauron and Saruman have attitudes similar to Denethor's in that they assume the impact of a person will match their appearance. The story of *The Lord of the Rings* completely inverts this expectation. The end of Denethor's conversation with Pippin illustrates this. Denethor only understands his misperception after Pippin explains the fuller story of the escape from the Orcs. Upon this realization, Denethor then admits, "looks may belie the man" (*LotR* V.1.756).

This powerful claim also advises readers to take a closer look before underestimating the seemingly ordinary. The ordinary hero may seem insignificant based on outside appearances, but the reality of their worth could be the exact opposite. A deeper and perhaps second or third examination of Tolkien's masterpiece is necessary to recognize how truly extraordinary the ordinary is. *The Lord of the Rings* invites us into a "merrier world" as we learn to treasure the ordinary — in the realms of Middle-earth and in our own.

Chapter 3

The Community Quilt
Britta E. Bunnel

WITHOUT A DOUBT, we live in an interconnected world. In 2016, Facebook analysts determined their average member — taking into account 1.6 billion people — was only 3.57 degrees of separation from any other user (BBC News). These connections are not limited to loved ones and peers but include strangers halfway across the world. We are all interconnected, and our lives are intertwined.

Tolkien's Middle-earth is reflective of our world and the threading complexities within it. There are intricate connections between inhabitants, and many readers are drawn to the interesting and important friendships. It is easy to be inspired by the loyalty between Frodo and Sam or laugh at the comedy of Gimli and Legolas, but these friendships do much more than simply entertain. They exemplify sacrifice and the appreciation of differences. They challenge us to build intentional relationships in our own lives.

Solely focusing on friendship would undermine the significance of the richness of connections in *The Lord of the Rings*. There are many types of relationships, each one serving its own purpose to advance the story and underscore its themes. Characters engage in a variety of connections and grow along the way, each person learning about themselves and their world. Witnessing character development reveals that Middle-earth is sustained by an interwoven patchwork of connections.

In Middle-earth, readers see a world filled with unity and camaraderie but also histories of brokenness and isolation. Although none of the relationships are perfect, nor are all models to follow, the interconnection of Middle-earth reinforces the value of seeking a diversity of relationships in our own lives.

Familial Connections
Family relations are foundational to a person's development yet are frequently overlooked. Unsurprisingly, this means the impact of these

relationships is dependent on the conscious efforts put into them, giving familial relationships the potential to be some of the most influential connections in one's life. C. S. Lewis writes that "family offers us the first step beyond self-love," providing the insight that family is our first opportunity to practice selfless and sacrificial love (*FL* 24).

Tolkien deeply valued family and wrote letters to his sons during the war to remind them of his love (*Letters* 46). In one letter to his son Michael, Tolkien writes that "the link between father and son is not only of the perishable flesh," suggesting an everlasting nature of family relationships (*Letters* 54). His consistent devotion to write to his sons communicates Tolkien's love even when the content of his notes was not always so expressive. These understandings of family connections as eternal bonds can be seen in *The Lord of the Rings*.

In Middle-earth, we often learn of heritage upon hearing a character's name. In introductions, Men, Elves, and Dwarves all include reference to their fathers: Aragorn is the son of Arathorn, Gimli the son of Glóin, and Legolas the son of Thranduil. Names carry cultural ties and show pride in one's family. Knowing and speaking one's name reminds each person that they are known, valued, and seen (Strauss). Declaring family titles emphasizes having pride in one's origin and the desire to bring pride to the family name. This leaves a direct impact on one's sense of identity and belonging.

The correlation between family and identity is seen in Hobbit culture. Hobbits delight in creating family trees and filling books with genealogies with vast, extensive connections (*LotR* Prologue.I.7). Each branch adds to the complexity of an individual's origin story (St. Clair 14). These trees and the stories they hold are glimpses of the deeply rooted familial values in the Shire.

The first family we encounter is the Bagginses. Bilbo and Frodo Baggins do not have a large family. Devin Brown points out that due to deaths of immediate family members and the broken relationships with extended family members such as the Sackville-Bagginses, Bilbo and Frodo only have each other (164). Their extensive time together allows Bilbo and Frodo to nourish their relationship. It begins to deepen upon Bilbo inviting Frodo to live at Bag End after Frodo's parents drown (*LotR* I.1.21). This sacrifice inherently brought Frodo into a close relationship with Bilbo as his provider. Without Bilbo's intentional, generous love for Frodo, the two may have remained disconnected relatives.

The depth of Frodo and Bilbo's connection is seen in their interactions when Bilbo embarks on a new adventure. Bilbo tells his nephew that the Shire has taken on a new sense of home, safety, and comfort, implying it is because of his relationship with Frodo (*LotR* I.2.62). We see Frodo reciprocating these feelings, as he desires to chase after Bilbo to stop him from leaving the Shire and their home (*LotR* I.2.62).[40]

Upon returning to the Shire after his own journey, Frodo feels displaced and like an outsider. He desires a safe place to heal from the wounds of the Ring, so he decides to leave the Shire again, but this time with Bilbo to travel to the West (*LotR* VI.9.1030). Their deep relationship persisted despite physical distance during Frodo's Quest. The Shire is no longer home for either Frodo or Bilbo. Their sense of home is found in the comfort of being together.

Éowyn and Théoden are also models of supportive family relationships. Théoden is Éowyn's uncle, but he endearingly calls her "dearer than daughter" (*LotR* V.6.843). Éowyn also carries this family devotion, and she loyally cares for her uncle while he is under Wormtongue's spell, despite their limited communication and his diminished personality (*LotR* V.8.867). Over time, Théoden and Éowyn develop a trust out of their intentional care for one another. They are loyal in a way comparable to the love among warriors who are fully committed to each other, willing to support one another no matter the trials (Catanach 2). This devotion explains why Éowyn is deeply distressed upon Théoden's death: her grief from losing him is so devastating that it causes illness (Johnson 118).

Family connections are woven throughout Middle-earth. As an example, Frodo and Merry are distant cousins. Although their friendship is potentially more influential than this blood relation, perhaps their connection is initially formed out of shared understanding of origin and context. We also encounter brothers Boromir and Faramir. Although we never see the two interact, Faramir conveys his deep pain upon finding his brother dead, telling Frodo that his "heart was filled with grief and pity" (*LotR* IV.5.666–67). In *The Hobbit*, we meet brothers Kili and Fili, the nephews of Thorin Oakenshield.[41]

---

[40] Another example of Frodo and Bilbo's closeness is in their shared characteristics. This occurs as a natural result of significant amounts of time spent together. Thus, it is not surprising that they are both pulled into perilous yet exciting adventures outside their comfort zones (Brown 164).

[41] I am indebted to David Bratman for his suggestion to include this point.

However, Kili and Fili are specifically called sister-sons rather than nephews. This distinct title emphasizes its importance, as the reference to "sister-son" signifies a deeper, innate loyalty to one another.[42] The three's closeness manifests in their commitment of giving their lives for one another, concluding with all three dying in battle, Kili and Fili defending Thorin to the death "with shield and body" (*H* 351).

Witnessing intentional familial relationships in Middle-earth illustrates the importance of remembering one's heritage and investing in family. When people isolate themselves, such as when Denethor distances himself from Faramir or in the bitter relations between the Bagginses and Sackville-Bagginses, they lose a source of innate tangible and emotional support.[43] Frodo and Éowyn's actions speak to their selfless care for their family members. Lewis's claims about family being the first opportunity to practice selfless love hold true in both cases. Perhaps both Frodo and Éowyn learn how to love others from the sacrificially loving relationships they have with their families. These healthy familial relationships serve as foundations of identity, sources of selflessness, and places of support.

Friendship
A superficial understanding of friendship is a comfortable relationship between people with similar interests. But this merely scratches the surface of all the potential found in friendship. Rather, friendship develops in many circumstances and takes many forms, and as a friendship grows, so do challenges within it.

Many philosophers have theorized about the virtuous benefits of friendship. Confucius calls friendship "profitable" when between those who are "true-to-death" or who have a depth of understanding about one another (205). But the question remains if these "profitable" friendships occur only for those with similar interests or backgrounds. Lewis writes that friendship arises when people recognize they have common "insight or interest or even taste which the others do not

---

[42] Honegger distinguishes between the relation of Kili and Fili to Thorin compared to that of Bilbo to Frodo. Frodo is actually both a first and a second cousin once removed to Bilbo, which they simplify with the term nephew, whereas Kili and Fili are Thorin's sister's sons. Honegger analyzes the depth of loyalty that Thorin innately has towards Kili and Fili using analysis of medieval cultures and the unique nature of a sister-son to uncle relationship ("'Uncle me no uncle!'" 6).

[43] For more discussion on Denethor and isolation, refer to Jung's analysis in Ch. 4.

share and which, till that moment, each believed to be his own unique treasure" (*FL* 65). Here, Lewis claims there only needs to be something shared in order to begin a friendship. Many friendships in *The Lord of the Rings* support this idea of common ground, but each one looks different from any other, and many develop in unlikely places.

Tolkien himself was largely influenced by friendship, demonstrated in his relationships with the Inklings, particularly with C. S. Lewis.[44] Diana Pavlac Glyer writes about the initial tensions between Lewis and Tolkien. Although their stark differences in opinion manifested in a series of "serious disagreements" upon beginning to work with one another, as time went on, the two were drawn together as a result of their shared interests (Glyer, *Bandersnatch* 11). They eventually became close friends, perhaps forming even stronger bonds as they learned to appreciate the differences between them.

Frodo, Pippin, and Merry share a friendship that extends past their antics. It exemplifies what Stratford Caldecott calls "a love for the other for [the other's] own sake" (*Power of the Ring* 178). Their relationships are sacrificial and — quite literally — "true-to-death." Although the friendship stemmed out of common interests, as the three grew up together and were often found adventuring through the Shire (*LotR* I.2.42), it is remarkable how different they are from one another in personality. These differences do not stifle their devotion to one another — they enhance it. When Frodo is about to begin his journey, Pippin and Merry insist on accompanying him to meet Gandalf at the Council of Elrond. They also refuse to be left out of the Fellowship, Merry telling Frodo that he "cannot trust [them] to let [him] face trouble alone" (*LotR* I.5.105). Impending danger does not impede Pippin and Merry from protecting their friend. They realize they are empowered together rather than alone, making it an easy decision to offer their lives for Frodo's sake (Caldecott, *Power* 172).

Pippin and Merry's devotion to each other is seen when Pippin finds Merry after the Battle of the Pelennor Fields and guides him to the House of Healing. Merry falls into Pippin's arms exhausted, and in that instant, Pippin's only concern is Merry's recovery (*LotR* V.8.858). Pippin's dedication to Merry is a reflection of the core of their friendship: selflessness. They uphold Lewis's perspective that in virtuous friendship, each person "feels humility towards the rest [...]

---

[44] I owe inspiration to include this paragraph to Paul Irwin.

and counts himself lucky to be among them" (*FL* 82). Pippin's actions express that Merry's needs are not burdensome and that it is an honor to be in Merry's company. Their relationship is an impactful example of lifelong friendship.

Cross-cultural friendships in *The Lord of the Rings* teach of the importance of overcoming natural differences to pursue relationships. Tolkien's legendarium describes Elves and Dwarves as naturally disposed against one another (*S* 44), and the relationship between Dwarves and Elves continues to be strained throughout history (*S* 234). This deep-seated tension pits Legolas and Gimli as unlikely friends, but it also allows for an enriched relationship that arises out of embracing differences and journeying together.

The relations between Dwarves and Elves can be analyzed using conflict theory. Conflict theory considers how groups of people who have specific interests based on their social positions may conflict with other groups (Barkan). It often pertains to classism and a growing sense of inequality between people over time. Conflict theory suggests that change can come as a result of groups learning from one another through their seemingly conflicting opinions. Change often does not easily occur, but acknowledging past tension and seeking to appreciate each group lay the groundwork to begin social change. Ultimately, conflict theory attempts to understand the role of conflict in creating social class tension and cultural clashes both historically and presently (Williams 34).

Legolas and Gimli's relationship shows this potential for change. At the beginning of their interactions, Gimli is proud of his knowledge of Moria and claims he does not need Elrond's elven-maps to navigate (*LotR* II.3.283). Some of this pride could simply be Gimli's gruff personality and communication style, but some may manifest out of his bias toward the greatness of Dwarves. It takes time for this deep-seated hostility to begin to break down.

Some of the differences between Legolas and Gimli are innate. In her research on Legolas and Gimli's relationship, Katherine Hatzfeld analyzed their natural differences, noting their communication styles have distinct rhythms and flows (Hatzfeld). Gimli's speech and song have a consistent rhythm, sounding like chants, whereas Legolas's speech carries a much lighter and "sing-song" quality (Hatzfeld). These undertones are generally characteristic of each of their respective cultures, adding to the differences between them.

Early on, Gimli and Legolas are often found bickering, and Gandalf implores them to move past their differences for the sake of the Fellowship (*LotR* II.4.303). But something changes when Gimli looks upon Galadriel's face, and while hearing her speak his language, "he looked suddenly into the heart of an enemy and saw there love and understanding" (*LotR* II.7.356).[45] Once Gimli recognizes the respect Galadriel, an elf, holds for him, a dwarf, he starts to shift his communication with Legolas from hostility into friendly banter.

Soon after, Gimli and Legolas compete for the highest count of orc killings at the Battle of Helm's Deep and tease one another without fear of offense (*LotR* III.8.534). In the midst of fighting, Gimli reminds Legolas that "there are enough [orcs] for us both" (*LotR* II.7.535). Legolas and Gimli are both committed to oppose Sauron and protect the good. Once they see past their differences, these shared interests are enough for them to become friends — even if it is sharing in killing orcs. This eventually transforms into a desire to understand and relate to one another (Moe 21).

Legolas eventually asks Gimli to speak of the beauty of Helm's Deep's caverns through his eyes (*LotR* III.8.547). This openness and sharing of stories indicate their comfort and trust (Moe 23). Although Legolas may not share Gimli's perspective, he intentionally asks Gimli to help him understand it. Their friendship proves that peace in any relationship is possible and leads to a friendship "greater than any that has been between Elf and Dwarf" (*LotR* App.A.III.1081; Moe 1).

Although the relationship between Legolas and Gimli is admirable, it raises the question of why their reconciliation was necessary to begin with. Middle-earth has been critiqued regarding Tolkien's design of hierarchies and races. One race, the Elves, are described as the most beautiful, being virtuous, immortal, and of light-skin (Baker 123). While reading Tolkien's works, it is clear that Elves are highly regarded and adored. Dimitra Fimi notes this in recounting how Elves developed from fairies into angelic beings who Tolkien favored (42). Fimi goes on to analyze how Social Darwinism and the "domination" of certain races may have influenced Tolkien in his creation of the hierarchy of Middle-earth (133). Although a full discussion on racism in Middle-earth is not within the scope of this chapter, it is important to acknowledge its presence and influence

---

[45] This observation can be attributed to Devin Brown.

on the story. The reconciliation between Legolas and Gimli is a significant element of the dynamics of the Fellowship, and it sheds light on Tolkien's convictions regarding friendship, but we need to consider its context rather than viewing it uncritically.

Intergenerational relationships can also come from unexpected places, as they are not often organic. However, these connections can still create long-lasting benefits. In a study that fostered short-term relationships between schoolchildren and senior citizens, the children were found to have an increased level of empathy and ability to communicate with the older generation, seeing fewer differences between themselves and the seniors than prior to their interactions (Hamilton et al. 237). In return, the senior citizens reported that contributing to the younger generation and connecting with the children was encouraging (Hamilton et al. 237). Even their short interactions left a profound impact.

Treebeard's relationship with Pippin and Merry exemplifies intergenerationality. As an Ent, Treebeard is part of the nature of Middle-earth and resonates with ideas of power and beauty (Aracil). Treebeard believes he knows everything about the history and beings of Middle-earth because of his life experience (*LotR* III.4.464). However, upon meeting Pippin and Merry, Treebeard does not recognize the Hobbit-kind (*LotR* III.4.465). As he talks with the hobbits, he realizes there are still aspects of the world he does not yet know. Treebeard's willingness to admit his lack of understanding is essential to his learning from the hobbits.

The hobbits are also unaware of who and what Treebeard is and approach him with timid curiosity. Much like children, Pippin and Merry initially judge him yet do not fear him (*LotR* III.4.463). Curiosity enables them to look past the generational gap and ask him many questions. The hobbits gather knowledge from Treebeard's experiences and share their own stories of Hobbits and everything happening in Middle-earth. The trio shares an immediate ability to listen intently and learn from the others' perspectives.

If a friendship is initiated out of intentionality, it will often break past barriers that initial differences may create. Both sides learn from one another and find joy in connecting with other generations. After the attack on Isengard, Treebeard jubilantly declares that Hobbits and Ents "shall remain friends as long as leaves are renewed," showing that he was not using the Hobbits as a tool for learning about the world and that he genuinely cares about them (*LotR* III.10.586).

In *Laelius: On Friendship,* Cicero analyzes the necessity of friendship and if that need is a source of weakness. Cicero concludes that friendship is an innate need of humanity, and that is why genuine friendship is vital to each person's well-being (*On the Good Life* 191). Friendships provide new perspectives of the world, especially when between unlikely pairs (Ruane and James 174). These differences encourage us to consider other ideas and grow as individuals.[46] Friendship teaches us what it means to be supported, supportive, thoughtfully challenged, and gently challenging. It is through friendship that we grow in our understanding of ourselves and the world.

Symbiotic Connections

Not all relationships deeply bond people to one another. Rather, some relationships are founded on utility, necessity, or convenience. These connections are often disregarded because they carry the connotation of taking advantage of another person. However, when both sides value the other for more than what they offer, there is potential for deeper relationship to develop. These are called symbiotic connections: relationships where both sides need one another.

Aristotelian philosophy acknowledges the dangers of friendships of utility. Aristotle claimed these friendships cease to exist as soon as they do not provide an advantage because they are founded on benefit rather than virtue (221). Aristotle called these friendships of utility imperfect because they are not rooted in virtuous living (Snyder and Smith 63–80). Since his version of utility friendships is built on an assumed selfish ambition, it follows that there may be wrong intentions in establishing relationships of this nature (Snyder and Smith).

Cicero approached friendships of utility from a different perspective, claiming some of his friendships that initially stemmed out of utility steadily deepened over time (*Cicero De Amicitia*). His analysis of many relationships revealed most were between "dissimilar partners bound together by bonds of utility and self-interest" (Snyder and Smith). He admitted that a connection founded solely on utility will be easily dissolved with the end of a need, but emphasized that love and respect in the relationship can sustain it past its utility phase (*Cicero De Amicitia*). Although there is danger of falsity in friendship

---

[46] See Ch. 1 for Kirkendall's argument about the nuanced perspectives given in the narrative by the literary technique of focalization.

and taking advantage of another person, Cicero pointed out that giving and receiving are always key "feature[s] and consequence[s] of friendship" (*On the Good Life* 191). What follows is this: if appropriate expectations are set for the nature of the relationship, there is still value found in relationships of utility. We see versions of symbiotic relationships such as these in Middle-earth.

Consider the relationship between a physician and a patient. A deep relationship cannot be assumed here, but there is still a need for a connection on both ends. The patient needs someone to help them restore their health whereas the physician feels fulfilled through serving the patient. A level of trust exists that allows the connection to potentially develop beyond its utility origin. Symbiotic relationships are not excuses to take advantage of another person, and they prove that connections of necessity are important.

Middle-earth is built on symbiotic relationships: alliances are created, fellowships are developed, and treaties are established in order to protect each nation and the people dwelling within. Mutual understanding in these connections leads to mutual benefit. With Cicero in mind, these connections can deepen into true friendships when thoughtfully invested in.

Alliances interconnect people and nations, and many of these agreements have lasted over the course of generations. Participation in international relations and fostering positive relationships lowers the probability of war because nations rely on each other (Ruane and James 79–80). Although some of these relations stem out of obligation, that does not lessen their importance. These alliances are crucial with the rising threat of Mordor, and Gondor must rely on its allies to come to its call for help during its siege (*LotR* V.1.770–71). When Rohan comes to Gondor's assistance, Théoden declares that "even if Rohan itself felt no peril, still [they] would come to [Denethor's] aid" (*LotR* V.3.799). Even in the face of almost certain defeat, these allegiances hold strong.

The answer to Gondor's call for help reflects the value of symbiotic relationships. Relying on one another is important, and the alliances in Middle-earth are upheld by balancing mutually beneficial give-and-take relationships (Ruane and James 89). The allies must be willing to come to one another's aid if they both want the benefit of protection. Although the allies of Gondor cannot bring enough warriors to outnumber the armies of Mordor, they bring the confidence that the people of Gondor will not be left stranded (Valente 34). By Aristotelian standards, this is not a perfect relationship because it is founded on utility rather than virtue. But without these alliances, there would not be any trace of hope for survival or victory over Mordor, making these symbiotic relationships critical.

The Fellowship of the Ring serves as another example of symbiotic connection. The Council of Elrond chooses the Fellowship's members to represent each of the Free Peoples of Middle-earth and each individual for their special skills to guard the Ring-bearer (*LotR* II.3.275). This is because it is necessary for Frodo to lean on the protection of the Company to keep himself and the Ring safe. The Fellowship protects him when traveling through the Mines of Moria and fighting off a Balrog and the orcs (*LotR* II.5.324–30) but also allows Frodo an opportunity to understand the Ring's power by guiding him to meet with the Lady Galadriel in Lothlórien (*LotR* II.7.360). These initially symbiotic relationships are invaluable to Frodo's mission.

The formation of the Fellowship prompts the creation of various relationships that quickly deepen into friendships. Cicero's claims are applicable here: intentionality cultivates meaningful relationships. Frodo certainly needs the protection of the Fellowship, but he undoubtedly prioritizes the relationships within it over his personal safety. He even tries to escape the protection of his friends in an attempt to keep them from risking their lives on his behalf (*LotR* II.10.406). The formation of the Fellowship serves as the reason for its members to come together, but these symbiotic relationships turn into friendships because each person is devoted to one another.

Although there is potential benefit in symbiotic connections, it is important to note they require careful engagement in order to be healthy. We see polar opposite sides of symbiotic relations in the dynamics between Frodo with Gollum compared to Gollum with the Ring.[47] Frodo and Sam capture Gollum when he tries to attack them and make a deal that Gollum will take them into Mordor (*LotR* IV.1.614–15). Frodo and Sam need Gollum because they do not know the way into Mordor, and Gollum needs the hobbits because they are in possession of his Precious, the Ring. Between Gollum and the Ring, Gollum needs the Ring; he is addicted to it. The Ring needs a being to manipulate, and Gollum was that being for many years. Here, the Ring needs Gollum to protect it from being destroyed. To compare these relationships, we

---

[47] Paul Irwin's suggestions inspired this insight.

need only point to the manipulation the Ring uses compared to the compassion Frodo extends to Gollum even upon betrayal. Frodo does not take advantage of Gollum and even protects him from harm (*LotR* IV.6.686) whereas the Ring controls Gollum, convincing Gollum he needs it to survive. This stark contrast makes it abundantly clear that though there can be richness in symbiotic connection, those rooted in manipulation should be treated with caution.

Symbiotic relationships can be overlooked but frequently impact day-to-day life. Ultimately, it is impossible for one person to do everything by themselves, which points to a universal human need: living in community and relying on one another. Thoughtful investment in symbiotic connections may even transform those relationships into genuine friendships. This alone should be enough to motivate us to lead with intentionality in relationships, particularly with the people to whom we are connected through circumstance or need.

Relationships of Complement
A person develops character when encountering new perspectives. If we are only surrounded by those with whom we share similar characteristics and opinions, we will always lack perspective. Developing connections with people who have understandings of the world unlike our own acts as a form of complementarity, or the idea that the differences that make two things opposites serve to improve both members (Guerrero et al. 73). Complementarity is not always reciprocally equal, but this does not lessen its value and influence. Investing in these connections requires vulnerability, but when done intentionally, cultivates support and understanding.

In the most traditional sense, master-servant relationships carry a negative connotation. This may be due to a history of abuse from master to servant or because they assume a detached connection between the two individuals. Although this stereotype is often found to be true, Frodo and Sam engage in a healthy connection of this nature. Perhaps this is because Sam joins the Fellowship purely out of sacrificial devotion to Frodo. As Frodo's gardener, Sam carries respect for Frodo and regards him as his master all the way to Mordor. Over the course of the Quest, Sam prioritizes Frodo's needs and protects him with his life (Greenwood 190). He carefully watches Gollum, ensures Frodo has everything he needs, forces Frodo to rest, and tells motivational stories. What sets Frodo and Sam's relationship apart is that Sam's dedication to Frodo and Frodo's response to Sam are reminiscent of a deep friendship more than a traditional master-servant relationship (Smol 955).

Sam and Frodo quickly grow close because of the circumstances they are forced into.[48] Much like the intimacy among those who have fought together in war, Sam and Frodo develop a closeness out of their need for support during a traumatic journey. John Garth analyzes Sam and Frodo's relationship in comparison to Tolkien's experience in World War I, in which Sam represents the privates and batmen, and Frodo symbolizes an officer (310). It is the shared experience of going through trials and trauma that brings the batmen and their corresponding officer — in this case, Sam and Frodo, respectively — into deep relationship. This closeness is reflected in Sam's agony over Frodo's trials and joy over Frodo's freedom from the Ring (*LotR* VI.3.947). Sam's servanthood transforms into sacrificial love.

Sam and Frodo learn from one another through their distinct yet complementary roles. Frodo leads their journey and becomes a role model for Sam. He tangibly teaches Sam about pity and mercy through his actions, particularly with Gollum (Nelson 18).[49] Sam's role is to care for his master and protect him. He teaches Frodo about perseverance, as he continuously picks Frodo up physically and emotionally, and pushes him to remember the mission (Nelson 18). Although exhausted upon reaching Mount Doom, Sam insists

---

[48] Some scholars argue that Sam and Frodo have a homosexual relationship. This argument is typically supported with evidence of the hobbits' "physical tenderness" and obvious emotional closeness (Smol 955). Conversations surrounding some of Tolkien's characters being queer, including Sam and Frodo, have continued to be relevant and are increasingly discussed. Support for these ideas include the argument that we simply cannot assume any character's cisgender or heterosexuality, and some characters, such as Frodo, already stray from the culture typically seen in their communities and may do so in other arenas in their lives as well (Petersen-Deeprose). Petersen-Deeprose also points out that the definition of queer is much broader than simply sexual expression, and it includes non-traditional emotional vulnerability and closeness. She asks readers to widen their scope of who may be included in this community from *The Lord of the Rings*. On the opposite end of the discussion, Lewis maintains, "kisses, tears and embraces are not in themselves evidence of homosexuality," and those who think friendship is a mere form of eros, or passionate and physical love, have never been in a true friendship themselves (*FL* 62). Both sides of the argument are thought-provoking, and the value of inclusivity and readers personally identifying with characters should not be undermined or forgotten.

[49] Dickinson discusses the concepts of pity and mercy further in Ch. 6.

that he carry Frodo up the mountain since he cannot take on the physical burden of the Ring himself (*LotR* VI.3.940). Frodo's gratitude is reflected in his relief over Sam being the one with him in the moments leading up to what Frodo believes to be the end of their lives (*LotR* VI.3.947). Sam and Frodo's complementary roles enable them to learn from one another and their different strengths and gifts. Servanthood and leadership are complements; although they appear to be opposites, they are a means to better the other.

Mentorship is also dependent on different roles within the relationship. For a mentee, mentorship provides an opportunity to learn from someone who has gone before them, while mentors pour into future generations and experience new perspectives themselves. This last element is critical: with mutually open minds, both mentor and mentee can gather new outlooks and grow in their characters. Both complement one another in bringing new opinions to the table for the other to learn from. We have a responsibility to share experiences with one another because "one's accumulated historically dusty and worn perspectives, can be the next one's fresh and inspiring life's set of invigorating insights and virtues" (Nystrom-Schut).

Gandalf and Aragorn are a non-traditional mentor-mentee pair. Gandalf has not directly acted in Aragorn's role before, but Aragorn's readiness to seek wisdom from Gandalf and Gandalf's willingness to share fulfills mentorship qualifications. Gandalf is of the order of the *Istari*, and, according to Middle-earth legend, was sent with fellow wizards like him "by the Lords of the West to contest the power of Sauron" (*S* 299). He is powerful in both "mind and hand" (*S* 300). Aragorn is eager to learn from Gandalf, recognizing his own impending ascent to kingship and trusting in Gandalf's wisdom (Hall 4). Through observation and conversation, Aragorn steadily learns from Gandalf and develops into a wise and discerning leader as a result (*LotR* App.A.I.5.1060).

Aragorn honors Gandalf's guidance by asking him to crown him on his coronation day. Gandalf agrees and blesses him as a worthy king (*LotR* VI.5.968). Gandalf's vast knowledge and Aragorn's authority as a future king act as complements to one another. Aragorn learns from Gandalf's wisdom and Gandalf is inspired by Aragorn's sacrificial leadership. Witnessing their connection proves the importance of investing in relationships with different yet complementary roles that result in mutual growth.

Romantic connections are perhaps the most complementary of relationships. It is not uncommon to hear that opposites attract, and with complementarity in mind, this is not surprising. When healthy, these relationships are deeply supportive, which can be attributed to a couple recognizing one another's gifts and needs. To Tolkien, the highest form of love is when the partners learn how to put the other's "desires, needs, and temptations" above their own (*Letters* 48). Although *The Lord of the Rings* is not of the romantic genre, the story would be incomplete without the romance found within. These relationships epitomize the power of sacrificial love.

The primary romantic connection in *The Lord of the Rings* is between Aragorn and Arwen. Although not much interaction is seen by readers, the two are deeply intertwined, and they marry in the end, speaking to the depth of their relationship as lasting through distance and time. Aragorn loves Arwen as soon as he meets her but is prevented from pursuing Arwen except from afar (*LotR* App.A.I.5.1057–59). However, his circumstances do not dampen his hopes of marrying Arwen one day. In fact, his pining serves as one of his motivations to continue battling evil and protect Middle-earth. Aragorn's affection for Arwen becomes his energizing force for the duration of the fight against Sauron (Nelson 9). When he finally becomes king and marries Arwen, it is the culmination of years of waiting (*LotR* VI.5.973).

Arwen decides to trade her Elven immortality for a mortal life with Aragorn because she does not want to live eternally without him once he passes away (*LotR* App.A.I.5.1061). The most meaningful part of Arwen's life is her relationship with Aragorn, and there is more life found in a relationship with him than in immortality. Arwen's choice demonstrates that sacrifice does not carry the same weight when it is for the person you care most deeply for. Even death does not feel like a sacrifice when it is for the person who makes you feel the most alive (Greenwood 174).

Years later, when Aragorn passes away, Arwen physically and emotionally grieves the loss of her beloved. Her grief causes her to lose the light in her face (*LotR* App. A.I.5.1063). Aragorn is Arwen's complement who brings that life to her eyes. Inherently, there is risk when letting one draw close to another's heart, and with this vulnerability comes the potential for heartbreak. However, if anything is worth that risk, it is love. Arwen's grief shows the beauty in recognizing how deeply one loves another, though there can sometimes be pain involved in that realization. Undoubtedly, love comes with its set of challenges, but these obstacles are trivial in comparison to the eternal gift of finding a complement and a companion.

Tolkien himself wrote about the deep devotion he had for his wife Edith in a letter describing their love story (*Letters* 47). Edith was his Lúthien, and she inspired the love story in *The Silmarillion* (*Letters* 420).[50] Upon Edith's death, Tolkien had "Lúthien" inscribed on her gravestone, making a declaration to the world of his love for her and her impact on his life. Their love overshadowed the struggles they experienced in their youth, as he describes the two rescuing one another from "sufferings of [their] childhoods" (*Letters* 421). Even if they were as different as Lúthien and Beren, an elf and a man, the two complemented one another. Tolkien's love-centered marriage impacted his life and writings, so though *The Lord of the Rings* may not revolve around romantic connections, this does not lessen their importance.

Relationships of complement take on many forms. Certainly, master-servant relationships are uncommon today, and not everyone chooses to pour into mentorship or pursue romance. However, relationships of complement illustrate the significance of seeking out and participating in connections where individuals differ. Complementarity can lead to character development and depth of understanding between people; it is this growth that compels us to seek out complements in our own lives.

A Connected Life

Without a doubt, relationships are threaded throughout Middle-earth. There is a rich history of pre-existing relationships prior to the journey, and we are invited to witness the cultivation of new ones over the course of the Quest. As a result, characters encounter new perspectives and learn to love one another well. They find encouragement, grow in character, and are supported beyond their ability to sustain themselves.

All connections vary in intimacy and impact, but intentionality is what transforms any relationship into one with purpose and significance. To be intentional in a relationship is to pursue meaningful

---

[50] Lúthien and Beren are at the center of the compelling love story in *The Silmarillion*. The two overcome the differences that naturally set them apart, as Lúthien is an elf and Beren is a man (S 162–87).

interaction. It does not automatically imply depth of understanding, but rather it simply means paying closer attention and interacting with thoughtfulness.

There is a richness of connection found in Middle-earth that must not be dismissed. Each relationship has the potential to be impactful, and not one should be ignored. Without any one connection between characters, the Ring would never have made it to Mordor and hope would have been lost. Characters needed one another and were emboldened together rather than alone.

The Fellowship is an example of the benefits of richness in connection. Without a unified mission, this group of four hobbits, two men, a dwarf, an elf, and a wizard never would have journeyed together. Each member of the Fellowship is unique, and there is diversity in the types of connections as a result. It is established out of symbiotic need but contains friendships, master-servant relationships, mentor-mentee connections, unlikely friendships that overcome past tension, and even extended family relations. Each person has a community to invest in and find support through. And though they do not physically travel together as a Fellowship for very long, their supportive relationships last throughout the journey, culminating in their joyful reunion upon defeating Sauron.

Middle-earth is not a perfect model nor a perfect depiction of relationships. There are many testimonies of connection that are excluded from the story, such as the pain in heartbreak, rejection in families, and histories of abuse. There is no such thing as a perfect relationship, and this remains true in *The Lord of the Rings*. The truth is that having connections does not make life easy or simple, but it does give it more purpose. We can still learn from imperfect connections and be challenged to seek out and improve relationships in our own lives.

Opportunity for connection is found everywhere, and a life lived without community is both lonely and challenging. When we feel disconnected from those around us, we quickly realize that experiencing wholeness is impossible without purposeful relationships. In studies comparing extroverts and introverts, it has been determined that every individual needs connections in order to be happy (Hills and Argyle 595–608). It is our responsibility to seek out connections and a privilege to experience their subsequent joys.

C. S. Lewis claims that the matrix of friendship is vital to the structure of community in society, and *The Lord of the Rings* highlights this truth (*FL* 63). Characters encourage one another and find support themselves. Relationships give us the opportunity to be fulfilled in serving others and to be served ourselves. Ultimately, we are not meant to live alone. We must seek community and rely on one another.

Connections are the threads that bring the pieces of the community quilt together and encourage the growth of individuals. The more intricately these pieces are brought together, the bigger and more beautiful the picture of community becomes. Tolkien does not write "Speak, friend, and enter" lightly (*LotR* II.4.306); these words not only open the dwarf-gate to the Mines of Moria, but they encourage the development of friendship and connection with those around us. Middle-earth reflects the value of community in our own world, inviting us to embrace a richness of relationship around us and allow ourselves to love and be loved by others.

Chapter 4

Restoring Broken Fellowship
Mark E. Jung

THE IDEAL LEADER is thought of as someone strong, smart, and charismatic — someone people look up to and are inspired to be. Traditionally, these leaders are pictured as heroes in battle and have the captivating charm to match. However, the strength of Aragorn's leadership comes not from his good looks or courageous fighting but lies in his ability to see the needs of others. His leadership is defined by selflessness and by building genuine relationships with those who follow him. Through this portrayal of leadership, *The Lord of the Rings* not only promotes the need for healthy relationships but also shows how leaders are critical in restoring broken connections.

Leaders as Stewards

The social structure in Middle-earth demonstrates a unique model of leadership, one that heavily involves master-servant relationships.[51] As such, characters are often defined by their status in relation to others. Colleen Donnelly highlights the "importance of the role of the vassal, the loyal follower, the everyman of medieval society" in Tolkien's vision of Middle-earth (18). These characters, including Sam, Merry, Pippin, and Beregond, are defined by their servanthood and fealty to a master, but they are nonetheless "true stewards and seconds — and it is on the backs of these characters that the true stability of society rests" (Donnelly 18). While Middle-earth's social structure is fundamentally based on hierarchy, Tolkien subverts this system by promoting stewardship. As Jane Chance writes, "The true king is a Steward, or servant, of his people" ("Power and the Community" 108). Thus, Tolkien exalts these characters of lower status to show how leaders are to serve others and restore community

---

[51] Look back at Ch. 3's section titled "Relationships of Complement" for a deeper exploration of master-servant relationships.

within society. His emphasis on these relationships demonstrates how good leaders are those who promote solidarity and community.

This is where Denethor fails as a leader: he is the only one with the title of Steward, but he fails to understand what that means. As Steward, he not only has the responsibilities of a master but is also a servant. Tolkien writes that a Ruling Steward is a "representative of the King during his absence abroad, or sickness, or between his death and the accession of his heir" (*Letters* 324). He is not the king, but his purpose is to serve the kingdom in anticipation of the king's return.

However, Denethor acts as though he is king. Denethor believes that he is entitled to unconditional loyalty because of his position of power. Donnelly writes that Denethor even has disdain for his son Faramir because "Faramir is willing to be a true steward and vassal" (23). He wants a son who is strictly loyal to him and does what is in his best interest instead of the best interest of those he leads.

Gandalf confronts Denethor and invites him to restore his status as Steward. However, in response, Denethor laughs in Gandalf's face and mocks him for having hope. Denethor rejects Gandalf's offer of hope and chooses to remain in despair instead. He believes what he has seen in the *palantír* to be true but does not know that he is being deceived. Donnelly comments that through the character of Denethor, "Tolkien demonstrates the destructive potential of those who cannot embrace the role of steward or vassal and who strive for a power that is above and beyond that assigned them" (18). He is not meant to use the *palantír* but is consumed by its power. Because of this, Denethor is in no condition to lead his people. He abandons all hope and refuses to give up authority and control, hoarding all his power and only looking out for himself. He rejects his role as Steward, and his people suffer because of it. Through Denethor's failure, Tolkien underscores how leadership can promote either community or isolation. Leaders have the choice to serve themselves or others.

In contrast, Aragorn's leadership is defined by prioritizing others and building relationships with those he leads. He cultivates community by fighting alongside those under him and exemplifying courage that inspires hope in the face of fear. Before going to the Paths of the Dead, Aragorn tells Gimli and Legolas that they should only come by their own free will because of the treacherous nature of the journey. Both agree to continue following Aragorn because of the love and respect they have for him (*LotR* V.2.781). Éowyn also shows her love for Aragorn by wanting to go with him and, although Aragorn denies her request, her loyalty to him shows the care he extends to those he leads (*LotR* V.2.785). Thus, Aragorn is an example of the ideal leader who cultivates genuine relationships with his followers and brings about unity within society.

Leaders as Redeemers

The relationship Aragorn cultivates with the Oathbreakers emphasizes the need for leadership as a means to serve and restore the marginalized. The Dead of Dunharrow are unable to die in peace until they are given the chance to be redeemed. Once known as the Men of the Mountains, these people swore allegiance to Isildur, but, because they worshiped Sauron, they did not come to aid Isildur in battle when he summoned them. As a result, Isildur cursed them "to rest never" until his heir would come to them and allow them to fulfill their oath (*LotR* V.2.782). Fulfilling the prophecy of Malbeth the Seer, Aragorn calls forth the Dead to fulfill their oath and ride with him and his company to drive away a fleet of Sauron's allies.

After their victory, the Dead are granted their freedom by Aragorn, who gives the command to "depart and be at rest!" (*LotR* V.9.876). He shows his authority as the heir of Isildur when he calls upon the Dead. Through his leadership, Aragorn gives the Dead an opportunity to fulfill their oath and finally have rest. When Aragorn calls out to them at the stone of Erech, he does not demand their assistance but instead gives them a choice. At the stone, Aragorn asks why the Oathbreakers have come, giving them the agency to choose redemption as they reply, "To fulfil our oath and have peace" (*LotR* V.2.789). Although the Dead of Dunharrow were cursed and separated from Middle-earth because of their failure to keep their oath, they are restored and given rest when they accept Aragorn's invitation to fight.

Similarly, Théoden reaches out to his followers, giving them the choice to follow him. Restored as king and in his right mind, Théoden extends an invitation to Wormtongue, offering him an opportunity to be restored despite his treachery. Théoden offers Wormtongue the chance to prove his loyalty again and ride with him and the rest of the Rohirrim to battle (*LotR* III.6.519). Théoden's actions emphasize how his own restoration allowed him to extend that invitation to others. This interaction demonstrates Théoden's desire to build community among his people and reach out to his followers, even those who have betrayed him. Even though he would be justified in killing Wormtongue, Théoden prioritizes unity over his own reactions and emotions.[52] It is this defining characteristic of his leadership style that rallies his people behind him.

A Fall Out of Fellowship

Aragorn's ability to cultivate unity and reach those who are marginalized is seen in full through his response to Boromir's failure. Before diving into Aragorn's strengths as a leader, we must explore the complexity of Boromir's disconnect from the Fellowship. At Amon Hen, Boromir falls victim to the temptation of the Ring and, in an act of desperation, tries to take the Ring from Frodo. His desire to save Gondor makes Boromir shortsighted, and he fails to see that there will be neither victory nor a Gondor to save if the Ring is not destroyed.[53] Boromir's plan to use the Ring does have a noble motive. However, it contradicts the purpose of the Fellowship, as Boromir chooses to prioritize Gondor over the Quest.

For Boromir, saving Gondor also means maintaining a claim to power. His inheritance of the stewardship depends on Gondor's strength to defend against Mordor, pointing to his incentive to use the Ring. Boromir's pride is twisted by the Ring's power; his motivation changes from a desire to protect and defend his country to a desire for power and glory for himself. This selfish desire is what ultimately leads Boromir to attack Frodo. He asserts that he needs the Ring but has no desire to keep it. But when Frodo refuses again to give it to him, Boromir rages, proclaiming, "It should be mine. Give it to me!" (*LotR* II.10.399). This is the culmination of Boromir's separation from the Fellowship. Boromir's attempt to take the Ring highlights how people can become corrupted and separated from society when they stop caring about the greater good, choosing only to elevate themselves and those close to them.

A Return to Fellowship

However, Boromir's restoration is just as significant, if not more significant, than his moment of weakness. This redemption is the

---

[52] See the section "Broadening the Scope" in Ch. 6 to read more on how mercy and pity play a role in this decision.

[53] See Ch. 5 and Paz's section on "Evil as Non-Being: The Clouded Mind" for more about the nature of the Ring and how it obscures reason.

result of both Boromir's choice and Aragorn's leadership. After Frodo puts on the Ring and runs away, Boromir cries out for him to come back. Boromir then returns to the rest of the Fellowship. His first step towards his redemption is the recognition that he did something wrong. He chooses to be accountable for his error, returning to the Fellowship when he could have fled. Despite being influenced by the Ring, Boromir views his failure as his own and takes responsibility for his actions.

Because he returns to the Fellowship, Boromir has the opportunity to be redeemed. Aragorn is the one who tells Boromir to go with Pippin and Merry, giving him the chance to be restored to his position within the Fellowship. Knowing that Frodo fled after an argument with Boromir, it would be reasonable for Aragorn not to trust him. Nevertheless, Aragorn chooses to continue to have faith in Boromir by giving him an opportunity for redemption.

Boromir takes advantage of this opportunity by protecting Merry and Pippin from the orcs. Linda Greenwood writes that Boromir "becomes a hero before his death," and his death acts as "a gift [...] to the very people (the Halflings) he had threatened moments before" (181). Through his death, Boromir is restored as the noble warrior he once was. He confesses to Aragorn about Frodo and the Ring before he dies, saying, "I am sorry. I have paid" (*LotR* III.1.414). Boromir's sacrifice and these apologetic words emphasize his repentance. He turns away from thinking only about saving Gondor and lays down his life for the hobbits. These hobbits previously seemed foolish from Boromir's perspective. They had no role in his plan to defeat Mordor with strength and might. However, Boromir's fall humbles him. He is able to see his own flaws and, in turn, to see the value in saving the lives of others.

From one perspective, it seems that Boromir has failed: he is killed when defending Merry and Pippin, and they are taken by orcs anyway. Yet this is when Boromir's own actions — his heroism and honest confession — contribute to his redemption. After hearing this confession, Aragorn affirms Boromir, saying that "few have gained such a victory" (*LotR* III.1.414). Here, Aragorn acknowledges Boromir's repentance and absolves him from his fall into temptation, inviting him back into fellowship and honoring him as a hero.

Some might assume that Boromir's redemption would require absolute protection of the hobbits and reconciliation with Frodo. However, Boromir fails on all these accounts. Still, Aragorn restores

Boromir because of his willingness to humble himself and value the lives of others. In Aragorn's eyes, Boromir was victorious. Tolkien scholar Sherrylyn Branchaw comments that when calling Boromir's actions a victory, Aragorn is referring to "Boromir's final realization of the wrong he has done, and his willingness to atone for it" (131). Despite his failure to save the hobbits, Aragorn exalts him because he is more concerned with Boromir's moral victory. Aragorn recognizes Boromir as a hero due to his sacrifice, restoring his status as a part of the Fellowship and honoring him by giving him a proper funeral. Through Boromir's death, Tolkien highlights both the agency people can play in their own restoration and the significant impact of leaders who reach out to bring the fallen back into community.

Restoration of the True King
Aragorn's journey to kingship itself stands out as a narrative of restoration. When readers first meet Aragorn in the guise of Strider in the Prancing Pony, they, like the hobbits, are unaware of his lineage and his right to the throne. The time before they reach Rivendell is significant as the hobbits get to know Strider, becoming his friend before learning about his true identity. During this time, Aragorn displays the same qualities he does later when he is recognized as the true king. He acts as a guide to the hobbits and promises that he will protect them, even if it means giving his life (*LotR* I.10.171). He also uses *athelas* to alleviate the pain in Frodo's shoulder after he was stabbed by the Nazgûl, demonstrating his healing hands (*LotR* I.12.198). Even without the title or multitudes of followers, Aragorn displays qualities of a true king, a king who stewards his people.

Leadership in *The Lord of the Rings* is intrinsically linked to healing and restoration. In the Houses of Healing, Aragorn uses *athelas*, also known as kingsfoil, to heal Faramir, Éowyn, and Merry from the brink of death. Aragorn's ability to heal is significant, as it is said that the true king will be known by his healing hands (*LotR* V.8.860). The connection between kingship and healing is emphasized further when part of Aragorn's healing includes calling others back with his breath and words. He first breathes on the leaves before crushing them, using the fragrance to heal Faramir. After waking, Faramir instantly recognizes Aragorn as the true king (*LotR* V.8.866). Aragorn affirms Faramir's loyalty and tells him to rest and prepare for when he will return to Minas Tirith. Aragorn then goes to Éowyn and calls her name as he uses *athelas* again to heal her. Lastly, Aragorn visits Merry and speaks his name as the fragrance wakes him. When he wakes, Aragorn calls him "Master Meriadoc" and makes jokes about not having his herbs to smoke, as he knows well that hobbits "use light words" in serious situations (*LotR* V.8.870).

In all three instances, Aragorn uses his speech as part of his healing process, which highlights the restorative quality of words. Faramir, Éowyn, and Merry are all on the brink of death because of the Nazgûl's Black Breath. It is the life-giving words spoken by Aragorn that counteract their suffering. Aragorn not only heals them from a near-death experience, but he is also aware of each person's needs beyond the physical, addressing each need in a genuine way that prioritizes the one he is caring for.

Aragorn's healing qualities as the true king are extended to the greater world of Middle-earth as he unites and restores kingdoms. Aragorn tells Imrahil and Éomer, representatives of Gondor and Rohan, respectively, that he is also known in Elvish as "*Envinyatar*, the Renewer" (*LotR* V.8.863). This name is appropriate — as Hammond and Scull put it, Aragorn is the one who "will restore the kingship in both Gondor and Arnor" (580). Throughout the narrative, Aragorn restores not only individuals but also people groups.

Even before he is crowned, Aragorn unites the Men of Gondor and Rohan along with the Dúnedain under his command. They stand together when Aragorn leads them to the Black Gate. Previously, Boromir thought they could beat Mordor with their military strength and the Ring. Now, directly confronting the forces of Mordor seems foolish as Aragorn stands in front of the Black Gate with fewer than six thousand men (*LotR* V.10.886). While Boromir's plan placed its hope in the might of Men joined with the power of the Ring, the hope for Aragorn's plan involves trusting in the mission of the Fellowship, fighting at the Black Gate in order to distract Sauron from Frodo's critical part of the Quest (*LotR* V.9.880).

Aragorn understands that there is immense danger for the army and gives them the choice of whether or not to follow him (*LotR* V.9.880).[54] Their plan is a suicide mission, but Aragorn's words show that hope exists even in the places of deepest despair.

---

[54] Refer to Paz's section "Weighing Evil in Middle-earth" in Ch. 5 for a closer look at this interaction and the way Aragorn acknowledges the weight of evil and fear.

Elrohir, Éomer, and Imrahil — leaders of the Dúnedain, of Rohan, and of Gondor — agree to follow and stand by Aragorn. They choose to follow him not because they believe the plan will succeed but because they are loyal to Aragorn and united by hope. This shows the influence Aragorn has and his ability to unify people even in the face of despair. Boromir was tempted by the Ring partly because of the great following it would grant him. Aragorn, throughout the narrative, certainly gains power; however, this was not the goal but simply a natural byproduct of his restorative and healing leadership.

Although he may not look like a king, Aragorn demonstrates the character of a good king from the beginning. He recognizes the stewardship inherent in true leadership and uses his authority to restore and unite those who are estranged. Aragorn also shows that true leaders are defined by the way they serve and protect others and not by their social status. Aragorn's leadership is not epitomized in his strength and valor but in the way he serves others and cultivates healing.

Chapter 5

Navigating the Weight of Evil
Hana Paz

IN THE LORD OF THE RINGS, readers follow Frodo and the Fellowship as they encounter living nightmares in their Quest to destroy the One Ring and stop Sauron from conquering Middle-earth. This plot summary divides the characters of Middle-earth into two categories: good and evil. This sorting is intuitive. The *Oxford English Dictionary* defines *evil* as the "antithesis of good in all its principal senses," with facets including "morally depraved," "vicious," and "doing or tending to do harm" ("Evil"). Sauron and his allies fit these descriptions of evil at every turn: they demonstrate only greed, pride, and violence. In contrast, the Fellowship and its allies are characterized by sacrifice, humility, and mercy.[55]

It may feel natural to say characters like Sauron, the Nazgûl, and Shelob are intrinsically evil; they appear to be evil through and through. Yet there are also characters like Denethor or Gollum who occupy a gray space somewhere between good and evil. Tolkien creates an intricate world, even in the way he develops the metaphysics of Middle-earth. Close inspection reveals a uniquely nuanced understanding of good and evil — one in which they are more alike in nature than most would expect.

Considering Dualistic Evil
If a reader opens *The Lord of the Rings* to a random page, they will likely encounter the actions and impact of dark forces. The Fellowship treks through sinister forests, encounters armies marching out of Mordor from the East, and hides from Black Riders and flying beasts that inspire terror. There are many resulting casualties. In "Mythopoeia,"

---

[55] Some characters, like Aragorn and Gandalf, demonstrate these qualities from beginning to end. On the other hand, Boromir grows into the virtue of sacrifice and Sam learns from Frodo to show mercy. Look to "A Return to Fellowship" in Ch. 4 for more on Boromir's sacrifice and to Ch. 6 for a discussion of mercy.

Tolkien writes: "and of Evil this / alone is deadly certain: Evil is" ("Mythopoeia" 88). This resonates with common experience in both Earth and Middle-earth. On Earth, people experience evil through betrayal and deceit, as well as acts of terror or genocide. The same is true in Middle-earth: Saruman betrays Gandalf, Gríma manipulates Théoden, and armies level towns and forests. The existence of goodness is also proven by experience, manifested in friendship, kindness between strangers, and humanitarian efforts. In *The Lord of the Rings*, the foremost examples of goodness are seen in the friendship and sacrifice of the Fellowship and the allies who loyally provide aid.[56]

Based on these observations, one logical conclusion could be that good and evil are *dualistic*, meaning that evil is an entirely separate force, distinct in nature from good.[57] In the field of Tolkien studies, Manichaeism is the dualistic philosophy most often applied to Middle-earth. Manichaeism states that good and evil are equal powers "locked in a struggle for world domination" (Davison 100). In *The Philosophy of Tolkien*, philosopher Peter Kreeft uses two Hindu gods to illustrate Manichaean philosophy. He explains that "Shiva the Destroyer is forever equal to Vishnu the Preserver" (174). In this understanding, both good and evil truly exist as separate, real forces from the beginning of time and they will coexist to the end.

Most notably, the benefit of a dualistic view like Manichaeism is its resonance with experience. It affirms that evil is an external force with universal impact. It simultaneously affirms that goodness is real, which can provide solace in the face of evil. In Manichaeism, the struggle against evil is brought to the forefront and described as an essential part of reality.

It is true that the evils in Middle-earth are tangible, yet dualism (and specifically Manichaeism) does not quite seem to fit. In contrast to the mythology of Manichaeism, Middle-earth has a primary, more powerful force: goodness, as embodied by Iluvatar. Maria Alberto helpfully points out that the creation story of Middle-earth, recounted in *The Silmarillion*, shows that "although Morgoth is the source of evil in creation, he is not coequal or coeval with Eru Iluvatar" (64).

---

[56] These themes are explored more thoroughly by Bunnel in Ch. 3, specifically in the sections "Friendship" and "Symbiotic Connections."

[57] Dualism refers to the general idea that, "for some particular domain, there are two fundamental kinds or categories of things or principles." Dualism does not exclusively describe good and evil, but it is a helpful term in this context (Robinson).

Moreover, a dualistic view holds that evil is as much a part of the fabric of the world — and the fabric of human nature — as good. There are beings and forces that are fundamentally separate from and opposed to good. In *The Silmarillion*, we learn that Illuvatar exists before creation and sings Middle-earth into existence. Morgoth is not a parallel creator; he is simply one aspect of the world that Illuvatar has made. When Morgoth chooses to rebel, he does not actually create; he merely takes one small part of creation and distorts it into something discordant (S 15–16). Tolkien's creation myth precludes any claim that good and evil are Manichaean forces in Middle-earth.

Even setting aside the origin of Middle-earth, dualism comes with troubling implications. If fundamental evil exists, then any "purely evil" creature could not be redeemed. The core of their being would need to be transformed from evil metaphysical substance to good metaphysical substance. Therefore, it is more difficult to explain the gray area that one also experiences between good and evil. Most troubling is the reality that, in a dualistic world, there could never be a resolution between good and evil. If good and evil have always coexisted and are equally real, they depend on one another. Good can never win. The struggle is indefinite and arguably meaningless.

Introducing Evil as Non-Being
Admittedly, a dualistic interpretation of *The Lord of the Rings* seems to align with experience. However, there are troubling implications that make it a less-than-perfect fit. This next perspective, that evil is best described as non-being, is counterintuitive. However, this philosophy allows for the complexity that makes Tolkien's depiction of evil so compelling.

Although "Mythopoeia" seems to support dualism by asserting that we are certain that evil is, it ends on another note. Tolkien describes that when those who resist evil finally reach the "Blessed Land," they will not see evil at all, because evil is "not in God's picture but in crooked eyes, / not in the source but in malicious choice, / and not in sound but in the tuneless voice" ("Mythopoeia" 90). Evil is not something innate but rather something secondary. It is in the eyes, not in the picture. If a dualistic perspective best represents reality, both evil and good would be a part of the picture. However, an understanding of evil as non-being holds that the most fundamental metaphysical reality is goodness — evil is something secondary, not inherent to reality itself.

Yet, in some sense, we are certain of evil's existence. Tolkien's complex understanding of evil is reflected in *The Lord of the Rings* and offers a nuanced alternative to dualistic conceptions of evil.

Evil as Non-Being: Diminished Nazgûl

A valuable counter to Manichaean dualism is the Augustinian philosophy that evil is best understood as non-being. This redefinition of evil requires a substantial vocabulary and paradigm shift. To facilitate this, we begin by looking at the Nazgûl for an illustration of how evil manifests in *The Lord of the Rings*.

The Nazgûl do not begin in a separate category of "evil." They are not made of a different substance from anyone else, but their original substance — their being — is made good and then corrupted by the influence of Sauron. The Nazgûl began as human beings with names, identities, and substance. However, after receiving Rings of Power from Sauron, they fall under the dominion of the One Ring. As a result, their very being is eroded: where there were once people, only Ringwraiths remain. Enslaved to the will of Sauron, they become devoid of any will of their own. Although they once had individual identities, those identities are completely subsumed in service to Sauron and bondage to the Ring. Although they once had physical bodies, they begin to walk in "the realm of shadows," physical in some respects but only seen in their true form by the one wearing the Ruling Ring (*S* 289). The Nazgûl are undoubtedly *less* than they were at the beginning of their story. Their being is diminished.

One of the changes from men to Ringwraiths that best illustrates their transition toward non-being is their incorporeality. The Nazgûl are visible only because they are draped with dark cloaks and sit astride dark horses or fell beasts, and so they are designated Black Riders. Their bodies are imperceptible. In her essay on incorporeality in Tolkien's *Lord of the Rings*, Yvette Kisor explains that "what seems so horrific in [the Nazgûl's] appearance is what should be there, but is not — it is the crown perched atop 'no head visible' and the laughter issuing from the 'mouth unseen'" (23). The corrosion of their being, manifested in their invisibility, horrifies other characters and readers alike.

The defeat of the Nazgûl completes the corrosion of their being. After Éowyn slays the Lord of the Nazgûl, the reader witnesses that the fallen armor and cloak are "empty" (*LotR* V.6.842). The Nazgûl is reduced to a "voice bodiless and thin" that rises into the air and fades (*LotR* V.6.842). Similarly, when Sauron's power is broken and his empire crumbles in on itself, the rest of the Nazgûl perish as well. Like flames extinguished, they "crackled, withered, and went out" (*LotR* VI.3.947). In these final moments, as their bodies disappear with what little existence still animated them, the reader can see how little good was left.

The Nazgûl provide a picture of the abstract concept that evil is *non-being*. This term contrasts *being*, which can be equated with existence or essence. These ideas are central to ontology: "the study of what there is, [...] what exists, what the stuff in reality is made out of" (Hofweber). Discussing evil in Middle-earth as Manichaean or Augustinian is to discuss the ontology of evil: not how it is defined, but what evil really *is*.[58]

St. Augustine of Hippo, a fourth-century church father, claims that the fundamental difference between good and evil is a matter of ontology. Augustine proposed that evil be understood as non-being, as nothing at its core (Hick 48). When something is defined by absence or loss instead of presence, it is called *privative*. Although this might be difficult to conceptualize, our framework of the world already accommodates similar ideas. Darkness is one example of this. No one can hold a handful of darkness because it is simply an absence of light. To define evil as "non-being" is to say that it is privative.[59]

The philosophy of evil as non-being is founded on Augustine's assumptions about the universe: God is good, and God is the foundation of existence. Therefore, existence is good (Coutras 126).[60] Ontology and goodness are essentially linked. Anything that *is*, anything that *exists*, must be good. In understanding this idea, it is helpful to apply the format of other privative definitions to evil. The verb *despair*, for example, is defined as "to be without hope" ("Despair"). If the state of being evil is defined in the same way, the

---

[58] This also differs from a discussion of ethics, which is concerned with good and evil as moral categories.

[59] Even though darkness and evil are privative concepts, it is still difficult to avoid talking about them as if they were forces of their own. Evil itself is an absence that must be named, just as dark is an absence of light that people have labeled. It would be clunky to always say "absence of light" or "not-light" when mentioning darkness. Similarly, it is difficult to avoid talking about evil as if it were an actor, though understanding evil as non-being requires that it cannot be one.

[60] Stated another way: "Existence itself is good, for it is derived from God's Being, the source and foundation of reality" (Coutras 126).

definition of evil would be "to be without good." Augustine would say that this is an impossible statement; nothing can *be* if it is without good, for *being* itself is good. Augustine scholar John Hick translates Augustine this way: "If the good is so far diminished as to be utterly consumed, just as there is no good left so there is no existence left" (48). According to Augustine, if there is no good, then there can be no being. Therefore, evil is non-being.

Does that mean that evil as we know it does not exist? That all the things we look at and label "evil" are illusory in some way? Certainly not. John Wm. Houghton and Neal K. Keesee explain Augustine's conclusion in this way: "Evil (as a Platonic idea, not individual evil things) is not an existing substance: for if it were, it would be good" (135). Augustine is not saying that individual evil things do not exist, but rather that "evil" as a concept cannot exist as a primary building block of the world. This idea, that good is a fundamental aspect of reality and evil is something secondary, radically changes one's worldview. Instead of a Manichaean world, where both good and evil are substances of the universe in a constant state of war, an Augustinian world is full of good — though parts of it are diminished, twisted, or lost.

Tolkien draws this important distinction in a note he wrote responding to a review of *The Lord of the Rings*: "In my story I do not deal in Absolute Evil. I do not think there is such a thing, since that is Zero" (*Letters* 243). *The Lord of the Rings* does not contain a character or event that fully encapsulates evil as non-being; that would be impossible. However, as the example of the Nazgûl demonstrates, Middle-earth functions as a world in which evil is privative — evil is a loss or absence of good, not a presence itself. The evils we can point to — both on Earth and in Middle-earth — are actually goods that have been marred by the non-being of evil.

It is these marred beings that make evil seem to have substance. Augustine scholar G. R. Evans explains that the forces we identify as evil are "damaged beings who are actively malevolent, exercising their wills for evil with a terrible energy" (99). The will is powerful when bent on destruction, demonstrated by damaged beings such as Sauron. Their impact makes it seem like evil does exist, although evil is nothing itself. For the Nazgûl, their decay is a manifestation of evil. Their power comes not from evil but from the good they started with.

Evil as Non-Being: The Clouded Mind

If evil is understood to be non-being, two things are necessary. First, every "evil" character is, in actuality, a good that has lost some goodness. Second, because evil is an absence of good, not an agent itself, evil itself cannot do anything. Only beings can act. Consequently, in order for bad things to happen, good creatures who still retain some being must become corrupted into agents of evil who do evil deeds. These two principles were demonstrated by the diminishment of the Nazgûl from human beings to Ringwraiths and the consequent damage they wreak. Another way that good characters fall is through the clouding of the mind.[61]

A clouded mind refers to a manifestation of evil that makes it impossible for rational beings "to think clearly or to see the truth" (Evans 104). As a mind is clouded, it becomes increasingly difficult to make coherent moral decisions. Hick explains that "Evil enters in only when some member of the universal Kingdom [...] ceases to be what it is meant to be" (47). In this framework, existence comes with moral responsibility. Therefore, a loss of that capacity is essentially a loss of being.

Sauron serves as a helpful illustration, as he is a good that has lost goodness. Elrond acknowledges that Sauron was not evil in the beginning (*LotR* II.2.267). In a letter to his publisher, Tolkien explains the process of this corruption — though Sauron begins with good motives, he starts "lusting for Complete Power" and is "consumed ever more fiercely with hate" (*Letters* 151). He is not evil by nature, but rather by fall.

This comes to pass precisely because Sauron's mind becomes clouded, and he renounces his purpose. Recall that Middle-earth was created by Eru Ilúvatar. Although Sauron is a Maia, a lesser divine creature, Tolkien writes that he "desired to be a God-King" and would have demanded that Middle-earth recognize him as such if he were victorious (*Letters* 243).

This results in our second point: Sauron is corrupted and becomes an agent of evil who oppresses Middle-earth. Sauron fits Evans's description well: he "act[s] upon the world in such a way as to twist everything [he] touch[es] out of its proper and good nature into something diminished or perverted" (Evans 104). Sauron is not non-being himself. He is a

---

[61] In this chapter, there is not a strong distinction between reason, will, and the mind.

powerful being who acts malevolently and harms others. However, this can only be true because remnants of his good origin still remain.[62]

Sauron's clouded mind is mirrored by Denethor. Perhaps it is easier to see that Denethor is a good person who has lost goodness, as he is less frequently characterized as evil to the same extent as Sauron.[63] Denethor was charged with the stewardship of Gondor, but when the reader meets him, he has lost this vision.[64] Although he claims he is focused on the good of Gondor, Denethor feels entitled to wield authority as Gondor's steward as if he were its king (*LotR* V.1.758; V.7.854). Denethor becomes increasingly misguided as he falls into despair and abandons his besieged city (*LotR* V.4.824). His clouded mind is most poignantly displayed as he attempts to kill himself and his son, despairing of possible victory and convinced it would be better to meet death on his own terms. Gandalf rebukes him, saying that this decision is not one placed under his authority. This insinuates that Denethor too has forgotten his place in the world order (*LotR* V.7.853). Although Denethor professes a commitment to good, he clearly carves a trajectory in the opposite direction.[65]

Saruman also veers from his created purpose, a fall that readers can see within the storyline of *The Lord of the Rings* itself. He begins as Saruman the White, the leader of the Council of the Wise, trusted by Gandalf and the Elves (*LotR* I.2.48; II.2.265). In his confrontation with Gandalf, Saruman argues that they need to rule over men in order to accomplish their goals (*LotR* II.2.259). Saruman, like Gandalf, is a wizard: one of the *Istari* (*LotR* App.B.1084). However, the pride that grew alongside Saruman's knowledge causes him to lose sight of this purpose and to vie instead for power over Middle-earth.[66]

---

[62] It is also significant to see these same patterns in the very first instances of evil retold in the legendarium. Accounts of both the fall of Melkor and the corruption of Sauron can be found in *The Silmarillion* (S 16–17, 31–32, 267, 385–90). Additionally, Maria Alberto's article "It Had Been His Virtue" deals skillfully with this topic.

[63] Denethor is noble and well respected before his fall. Even so, the qualities that predisposed him to fall, namely his pride, are demonstrated in his response to Gandalf when he visits Gondor to research the Ring (*LotR* II.2.252).

[64] For a closer look at Denethor and the role of stewardship, refer to Jung's section on "Leaders as Stewards" in Ch. 4.

[65] Both Augustine and Tolkien believed that anyone who does evil deeds is convinced that they are moving toward good. Tolkien writes, "many still need to have 'good motives,' real or feigned, presented to them" (*Letters* 242).

[66] Harbman looks at Saruman's lust for power through the lens of disenchantment in Ch. 8.

Although a less severe case than either Saruman or Denethor, Boromir is a tragic example of both the consequences of a clouded will and the Ring's power to cloud it. In his zeal to protect Gondor, Boromir loses clear sight of reality. He is convinced that it is his right to wield the Ring and that it cannot corrupt him, nor any "True-hearted Men" (*LotR* II.10.398). There is no such evidence in the history of the Ring, and his conviction ignores the Ring's effects on its bearers, as well as the origin of the Nazgûl. Houghton and Keesee explain that the corrupting power of the Ring functions "so that [the bearer's] desire for goodness becomes instead the desire for domination" (143). Out of this confused desire for domination, Boromir tries to take the Ring from Frodo. Boromir immediately realizes his error when Frodo flees. Boromir describes that a "madness" came over him (*LotR* II.10.400). He recognizes that his mind was clouded. Because of the Ring, he is unable to see goodness clearly.

These characters all demonstrate the understanding of evil that Augustine describes. Evil is not a substance of its own but a lack of what is natural and good. These characters begin with wills that are directed toward goodness, yet they turn away to varying degrees.[67] Because of their clouded minds, they take on the role of the forces of evil in Middle-earth: Sauron, by his attempted world domination; Denethor, by his neglect and attempted murder-suicide; Saruman, by his destruction of nature and opposition to the Company; and Boromir, by attempting to take the Ring and speeding the splintering of the Fellowship.

Evil as Non-Being: What Has Been Twisted
There are some evils in *The Lord of the Rings* that seem glaringly inconsistent with the idea of evil as non-being. Shelob, the spider-like creature that Sam and Frodo encounter on their way into Mordor, is horribly substantive. Her existence is challenging. It seems that she might be an example of dualistic evil, an entity separate from good. Looking back at her origin seems to confirm this: her ancestor, Ungoliant, has an incredible power of darkness. *The Silmarillion* tells that "she sucked up all light that she could find" and wove it into "Unlight, in which things seemed to be no more, and which eyes

---

[67] The legendarium explains that the nine men who become Nazgûl fall at varying times based on their "native strength" as well as the condition of their wills (*S* 289).

could not pierce, for it was void" (*S* 73–74). This describes Unlight not as a privation of light, but as an active negation of it.

Although this darkness seems to contradict a philosophy that defines evil as non-being, it is not necessarily opposed. Note that Ungoliant consumed light to form Unlight; she did not make it out of nothing (*S* 73). The root of Unlight is a good substance: light. Coutras explains, "This evil is not the *lack* of light but rather its desecration. [...] It is an absence of light, as well as a darkness made out of light" (128). What is commonly called evil is not only the absence of good but the twisting and perverting of something good into something less good. Unlight is an extreme example of this.

Moreover, Unlight is described as "void." It is crucial to remember that void was in the beginning before the creation of Middle-earth, not as something evil but as something not-yet-made (*S* 15). Void, therefore, is the most extreme lack of substance possible — it is truly evil in the Augustinian sense.

It is less clear how Ungoliant herself fits into the philosophy of evil as non-being, since her origin, as recounted in *The Silmarillion*, is uncertain (*S* 73–74). However, this lack of explanation leaves space to apply a consistent philosophical framework throughout the legendarium: that she also began as something good before she was corrupted into darkness. The end of Ungoliant further aligns with a philosophy of evil as non-being. *The Silmarillion* retells a legend that her insatiable hunger for light finally resulted in her devouring herself (*S* 81). In that case, she is one of the clearest pictures of privative evil: non-being reaches its final end, and she is reduced to nothing.

Although Shelob is one of the most tangible manifestations of darkness in *The Lord of the Rings*, looking back at her ancestor Ungoliant reveals their shared connection to non-being. Shelob carries the same greed and hunger that eventually reduced Ungoliant to nothing. She is generationally affected by the twistedness of her ancestor. Yet Shelob's very existence shows that there is something of goodness that remains.

Treebeard speaks similarly about the trolls, saying that they were twisted by the Enemy to mock the Ents (*LotR* III.4.486). These creatures that would generally be called "evil" are not examples of dualistic evil; they are not separate evil beings. Instead, they manifest the non-being of evil in a way radically different from the Nazgûl: they are twisted beyond recognition.

The Weight of Evil

And yet, despite the privative nature of evil, real damage is caused by agents of evil. This reality cannot be dismissed. Loss of life, freedom, or security — though these are privations — all deserve to be recognized and grieved as the tragedies they are. Unfortunately, the philosophy of evil as non-being can lead some people to dismiss the experiences of evil as unimportant in comparison to the primary reality of good.

Tolkien and his contemporaries did not dismiss the weight of evil. Tom Shippey writes that twentieth-century authors, including Tolkien, were faced with a disturbing contradiction between their compelling current experience of evil and the accepted philosophies of the past. Shippey states that their experiences "left them with an unshakable conviction of something wrong, something irreducibly evil in the nature of humanity, but without any very satisfactory explanation for it" (*Author* 121). This is an understandable conviction. The twentieth century brought new weapons of cruelty and destruction during two major World Wars; Tolkien fought in the first and watched his sons fight in the next. As genocide, violence, and bids for world power swept across Europe, it is no wonder that Tolkien and his contemporaries wrestled with the traditional answers they had been taught, which were more in line with Augustinian philosophy.

Tolkien's reaction to this problem is to emphasize experience as a facet of reality that is as important as the less tangible truths of philosophy. Recall the excerpts from "Mythopoeia." Before the lines stating that evil is "not in God's picture but in crooked eyes," Tolkien writes that we are "deadly certain: Evil is" ("Mythopoeia" 90, 88). Although paradoxical, both being and experience are necessary facets of reality. To have either without the other results in a distorted perspective. To discount experience is to deny or gloss over the suffering that comes at the hands of evils, minimizing the weight of grief that it deserves. But to discount the reality of evil as non-being is to miss out on the hope that comes from this understanding, to deny the danger of good's corruption and the possibility of its redemption. *The Lord of the Rings* not only illuminates the ultimate reality of evil as non-being but also affirms our deadly certainty that evil is.

Weighing Evil in Middle-earth

On the way to Helm's Deep, a large silhouette obscures the moon, and the men are beset by a blind fear and biting cold (*LotR* III.11.595).

Without making a noise, without even coming close, the Nazgûl's weapon of fear accosts the riders below. The experience of terror and despair that the Nazgûl incites is not dismissed but is viscerally described on multiple occasions.

When the hobbits flee the Shire, still unaware of what the Nazgûl are, they encounter a group of elves, led by Gildor. The elves immediately agree, against their custom, to travel with the hobbits when they hear that the hobbits are being pursued by Black Riders (*LotR* I.3.80). Moreover, Gildor refuses to tell Frodo more about these creatures, both because he does not think it is his place and because, if he did tell them, terror might keep the hobbits from their Quest (*LotR* I.3.83). The experience of evil here is recognized and acted upon — the threat of the Black Riders and the terror they would instill in the hobbits both matter.

Throughout the Quest, fear is not dismissed in favor of hope; instead, fear is recognized as a powerful weapon. The One Ring is another Tolkienian manifestation of evil that is uniquely experiential. In Mordor, Sam takes up the Ring when he thinks Frodo has died. As he enters the tower where Frodo is kept, he comes face-to-face with an orc and clasps his hand around the Ring. The narrator tells readers that the orc sees a large, intimidating shape instead of a terrified hobbit (*LotR* VI.1.904). Even though the orc cannot see the Ring held in Sam's hand, and even though it poses no real danger, the orc perceives a terrible, hidden power and he flees (*LotR* VI.1.904). Fear goes before the evils in Middle-earth, a weapon that amplifies whatever power they have.[68]

Aragorn demonstrates the value placed on the experience of evil. As the Captains of the West and their forces make their final march to the Black Gate, the fear of the Nazgûl couples with the seemingly hopeless outlook of the battle to produce incapacitating terror in some soldiers (*LotR* V.10.886). Aragorn, instead of dismissing their fear and encouraging them with an appeal to a greater reality, pauses in the weight of their experience. He understands them and has compassion on them. He knows that they are walking into their worst nightmare made real (*LotR* V.10.886). In view of this, Aragorn gives them an opportunity to turn back with honor and fight enemies under less

---

[68] When Legolas recounts the way that the Dead took the ships from the enemy, he admits that he is not sure whether their shadowy swords would have any effect — they never had to use them, for their foes simply fled in fear of them (*LotR* V.9.876).

dire conditions.[69] Some, impacted by the mercy he offers, subdue their fears and remain. But others are encouraged by the thought of being able to accomplish some good and leave (*LotR* V.10.886). In providing them this opportunity, Aragorn affirms the weight of the experience of evil and, in doing so, validates their fear — their experience of evil — as a meaningful facet of reality.

Throughout *The Lord of the Rings*, some characters begin to despair when tragedy strikes and they experience evil. The tendency toward despair is dealt with artfully. These moments are not glossed over but are instead given pause: there is space for sorrow and grief, for doubt and fear. Tolkien does not rush the reader, nor his characters, into hope.

Paragraph breaks provide noticeable opportunities to pause and emphasize the validity of experience. As Pippin and Beregond sit in Gondor with the forces of Mordor closing in around them, they consider whether there is any hope that Gondor will stand. As Pippin remembers the varied evils he has encountered, a Nazgûl cry resounds, and the paragraph ends with Beregond feeling that even the warmth in his blood has been stolen (*LotR* V.1.766). At that point, there is a paragraph break, a blank line where the weight of this experience can set in.

And then a new paragraph begins. Pippin looks up and sees the sun shining and the banners waving, and he shakes himself. He recalls Gandalf's miraculous return and denies despair. He declares that they will stand, even if only on one foot or on their knees (*LotR* IV.1.766). This encouragement, this movement toward hope, is neither naïve nor dismissive. It occurs only after the weight of evil is recognized. Even after this moment, Pippin expresses that he wishes the war were over all the same (*LotR* IV.1.766). Such moments of pause between paragraphs of despair and hope occur throughout the narrative.[70] The tangible experience of evil matters, but it is not cause for despair.

In fact, the experience of evil often pushes characters forward even when hope is lost. When Éomer sees the body of his sister Éoywn, who he presumes is dead, he rides out with renewed energy, leading a chant for death and ruin (*LotR* V.6.847). The resurgence of strength is not due to hope but due to pain and anger, a response to the evils he has endured.

---

[69] Look to Ch. 4 for a closer look at Aragorn as a restorative leader.

[70] Some examples include a moment during Merry's march with the Rohirrim and a moment for Sam after Frodo's apparent death in Mordor (*LotR* V.5.837; IV.10.731).

People who fight for the preservation of their own lands also fight because of the experience of evil and a desire to prevent that loss, fear, and pain from affecting their own people. Fangorn Forest suffers under the corrupted rule of Saruman. When Treebeard recounts his experience of loss, readers feel the sorrow along with him. He laments the lost voices of the trees that Saruman destroyed, his friends whom he had known from their infancy as acorns. He cries, "It must stop!" (*LotR* III.4.474).

The weight of experience spurs the characters in *The Lord of the Rings* to fight and resist, to push back against evil — not because of what it *is*, but because of what it *does*.

Space for Hope
In the face of what evil *does*, a right understanding of what evil *is* has crucial implications. First, a new understanding of evil as non-being requires a new understanding of how it can be defeated. Sauron and Saruman have resources that the Free People cannot compete with. Yet, these dark forces are ultimately defeated not by strength but by ordinary courage, friendship, and commitment.[71] This outcome challenges not only traditional conceptions of evil but also traditional conceptions of strength.

Second, the response to evil characters changes. If a dualistic philosophy is true, then evil is a distinct substance, foreign to good characters. Therefore, disgust and annihilation would be reasonable responses to all evil creatures. If evils are actually perverted goods, then there is room for pity. This right response is powerfully illustrated through Bilbo, Gandalf, Frodo, and eventually Sam as they interact with the wretched creature Gollum. Since every evil character is a good that has been lessened, there exists the possibility of reform, repentance, and healing.

Third, *The Lord of the Rings* leads to a better understanding of the danger of privative evil: good is corruptible and corruption has fatal consequences. The Ring must be taken seriously because it overcomes the good beings who try to use it. Boromir is one example of this possibility. His desire to help Gondor, noble and honorable in itself,

---

[71] This is perhaps most strongly demonstrated by the Fellowship and specifically by the hobbits. Mar discusses the unassuming power of Hobbits more fully in Ch. 2.

is twisted and results in his attempt to take the Ring from Frodo by force (*LotR* II.10.399). Boromir demonstrates the danger of corruption.

Finally, and most importantly, reflecting on the non-being of evil can lead to a hope that is not circumstantial, a hope that is instead drawn from knowing the primacy of good. In Mordor, Sam experiences this hope in the middle of an incredibly hopeless situation. After Sam reaches an apparent dead end while looking for Frodo, he sinks down in defeat. Suddenly, prompted by something in him that he cannot quite identify, Sam begins to sing. As he sings of the Shire, his strength grows and culminates in a song of his own creation. He sings of the sun above the shadows and refuses to say that day is over (*LotR* VI.1.909). This song of defiance strengthens him — and ultimately leads him to Frodo, who cries out in response. The reality of the good that transcends his experience gives Sam the will and ability to keep going.

This is amplified when Sam looks up at the night sky and sees a single white star. Looking at it, he is struck by its beauty, and his hope is revived. He realizes that "in the end the Shadow was only a small and passing thing: there was light and high beauty forever beyond its reach" (*LotR* VI.2.922). This hope does not come from a change in his or Frodo's circumstances but in the overarching reality of good, a good that is more real than evil could ever hope to be. Sam sleeps soundly that night, though he must still face the horrors of Mordor in the days that follow.

Stated simply: if evil is non-being, then there is hope.

Navigating Evil with Hope

Middle-earth reflects our own world in many ways, and it is worth considering what it might mean if what is true of evil in *The Lord of the Rings* is true of evil in our own lives. The experience of evil compels action because there is good worth protecting. Even so, in a world inundated with painful experiences and global crises, it can feel like fighting for good is a useless endeavor. A dualistic view only amplifies that sensation. However, understanding that evil is not a force of its own can provide an anchor of hope. This is not always something we can feel, as Sam feels hope in Mordor. Instead, hope may seem incredibly distant. Holding the tension between experience and philosophy is a practice that requires strength, awareness, and vision.

Gandalf provides this kind of vision by the way he navigates both the truth of the privative reality of evil and its seemingly contradictory strength. In front of Gondor's gate, Gandalf commands the Lord of the Nazgûl: "Fall into the nothingness that awaits you and your Master" (*LotR* V.4.829). This suggests that Gandalf has confidence in his knowledge of the nature of evil and its ultimate end.

Although he knows that Sauron's power is less than fear makes it seem, this does not cause him to dismiss evil. Gandalf also must fight to maintain hope when faced with tangible manifestations of evil. He admits at the Council of Elrond that he faced great fear when he was trapped in solitude in Isengard — it was difficult for Gandalf to imagine that Frodo could prevail over the Black Riders (*LotR* II.2.261). Additionally, after their arrival in Minas Tirith, Gandalf and Pippin hear news from Faramir about Frodo and Sam's journey. Pippin asks Gandalf directly if there is still hope. Gandalf answers, "There never was much hope" (*LotR* V.4.815). He mutters in distress about Frodo and Sam's course toward Shelob.

However, he continues that "in truth" he believes this news does have some hope in it (*LotR* V.4.815). Although Gollum might intend harm for the hobbits, Gandalf holds on to the knowledge that good can come unintentionally, even from acts of betrayal. This conversation demonstrates that finding hope amidst the experience of evil is difficult even for Gandalf, despite his unique closeness to the nature of Middle-earth as one of the *Istari* and his knowledge that evil is privative.[72]

In navigating this tension, Gandalf shows a capacity to feel the weight of experience without giving it significant power. Gandalf is empathetic when Denethor is grieving the real trauma of his son's death. Yet he is not silent when Denethor is ungracious to Faramir. Gandalf rebukes him, saying "Be not unjust in your grief!" (*LotR* V.1.755). It is healthy to grieve, to acknowledge pain, but it can be detrimental when allowed to rule over life.

Neither does Gandalf permit the non-being of evil to be an excuse for inactivity or for ignoring the harm caused by evil. Before they march to the Black Gate, Gandalf says that all they can do is "[uproot] the evil in the fields [they] know" (*LotR* V.9.879). It is impossible to preemptively solve what evils might come in the next age, but there are agents of evil that need to be dealt with now and corruption that needs to be remedied today.

---

[72] Gandalf's understanding of the nature of Middle-earth is hinted at during his confrontation with the Balrog (*LotR* II.5.330).

We also must do what we can, in the time we find ourselves in, with the evils we can confront. But the hope of the deeper reality, the hope of knowing that all of being is good, is that there is light far above the shadow of evil. Gandalf knows that the entire weight of experience, the responsibility for it, does not fall on him. There is a force of good greater than any of us alone or even all of us together.

Chapter 6

Making the Risky Choice
Anna K. Dickinson

BOTH THE FIRST-TIME READER and the Tolkien veteran know that Gollum creates problem after problem throughout the Quest to destroy the One Ring. He is slimy, deceitful, and corrupt. Gollum is perplexing; he is as ugly as can be, but readers are still captivated by his character. Although he is no traditional hero, Gollum inadvertently saves the day when he wildly bites off Frodo's Ring-wrapped finger before tripping into the furnace of Mount Doom and perishing along with the Precious (*LotR* VI.3.946).

It might be that Gollum is memorable because his final moment is so haunting. Or maybe something about his character speaks to us at a deeper level.[73] Some scholars think that Gollum fascinates us because in some way we identify with him (Arthur 25). Perhaps, in Gollum, we actually see ourselves. He experiences loss and suffering, straying significantly from his true identity as Sméagol. He trades relationships for self-interest, leading to his demise. We feel the weight of those same struggles: we lose our way, become caught up in the wrong things, and consequently ruin relationships. Perhaps this is the intrigue of Gollum's character.

Or maybe it is Gollum's integral role in the destruction of the One Ring that so firmly captures our attention. His selfish intent leaves room for the good to prevail, demonstrating that even the wrong decision can bring about the right outcome, and this surprises us. Regardless of the reason, Gollum lingers in our memories, and his complicated role allows for several compelling themes that permeate the story.

Throughout *The Lord of the Rings*, none of the characters feel any particularly positive emotions toward Gollum. Not even one of

---

[73] Andy Serkis's portrayal of Gollum in *The Lord of the Rings* movies is worth noting. More likely than not, part of the reason why Gollum is so memorable is because Serkis did such a remarkable job portraying him in the movies.

them grieves his death.[74] However, Gollum's story is punctuated by instances of pity and mercy that keep him alive until the most crucial part of the Quest. Through the storylines of Gollum and many other characters, Tolkien weaves pity and mercy into *The Lord of the Rings*, reflecting the way they are also intricately woven into our own world.

Tolkien's Perspective on Pity and Mercy
The Middle-earth that readers encounter in *The Lord of the Rings* is backed by extensive history and lore. Part of Tolkien's meticulous, lifelong development of this world stemmed from his fascination with and passion for language. A philologist through and through, Tolkien had remarkable command of the English language and its history, and this rootedness inspired the invention of many languages (Carpenter, *Biography* 42–44).

With Tolkien's purposeful wording in mind, it is noteworthy that pity and mercy are occasionally capitalized in *The Lord of the Rings*. This happens specifically when Gandalf uses these terms (*LotR* I.2.59). Tolkien's emphasis, expressed in Gandalf's voice, is clear. To a modern reader — particularly an American one — the use of the word pity might come as a surprise since a modern cultural understanding of pity often implies looking down upon another's pain in a condescending manner (Ducey 300). While this self-focused act of looking down on others can be a component of pity, Tolkien's work approaches this word from an entirely different angle. Instead of pity being selfish and demeaning, pity in *The Lord of the Rings* is contrary to personal benefit and devoid of pride. We can consider this kind of pity to be similar to empathy.

Tolkien's perspective on the term can be gleaned from his belief that pity "must restrain one from doing something immediately desirable and seemingly advantageous" (*Letters* 191). By this definition, pity prohibits the seemingly obvious, quick, and beneficial act. Rather, it involves a choice that makes less logical sense, takes more time, and does not guarantee an advantageous outcome. The way

---

[74] I owe this insight to Mary K. Ducey. Some may argue that Frodo's decision to forgive Gollum in the aftermath of their interaction on Mount Doom indicates grief over Gollum's death (*LotR* VI.3.947). However, in reviewing this chapter, David Bratman pointed out that, although these words are closer to a eulogy than anything else said about Gollum, they by no means reflect any deep mourning surrounding his death.

Tolkien writes about it, pity is a choice that avoids dismissing another person's pain and instead compels us to consciously slow down and let that pain affect us. Pity is neither an emotion nor an action. Instead, it is a posture that requires active presence in a situation to allow its gravity to take effect. It is compassion, not superiority; respect, not disdain. Pity does not put an immediate end to negative feelings, but it can cause us to take the time to acknowledge someone else's story and experience. This often leads to merciful actions.

Mercy, distinct from pity, is also important in understanding *The Lord of the Rings*. All throughout the text, the theme of mercy persists. It is implicit to the storyline, not standing out as an overt lesson in morality but subtly demonstrating the power and significance of merciful actions. In his letters, Tolkien acknowledges that mercy is part of "Divine nature," and, given his Catholic faith, a Catholic understanding of this word is both helpful and important (*Letters* 326). The Catechism of the Catholic Church defines mercy as "compassionate sorrow at another's misfortune together with a will to alleviate it" (*New Catholic Encyclopedia* 504). Tolkien's works explain that mercy not only sees pain and chooses to feel it but also seeks to do something about that pain. Furthermore, the word mercy often connotes compassionate action toward one who deserves punishment ("Mercy"). Mercy takes deliberate empathy and moves beyond it to action — even when that action is undeserved.

Tolkien expands upon the concept of mercy by clarifying that true mercy is selfless. In one of his letters, he defines mercy as the "supreme value and efficacy of Pity," indicating that mercy acts on pity (*Letters* 252). However, Tolkien is adamant that people cannot extend mercy simply because it could produce personal benefit. Rather, he clarifies that mercy for self-centered purposes is not mercy at all but selfishness. Tolkien's argument is not that "one must be merciful, for it may prove useful later" (*Letters* 253). Instead, he makes bold claims about the riskiness of mercy. By definition, mercy should not be rational but should be "contrary to prudence" (*Letters* 253). It is not cautious. It is quite reckless and requires great courage. Therefore, mercy cannot be self-seeking. Instead, it is self-risking and self-negating.

In *The Lord of the Rings*, many obvious examples of pity also include mercy, and vice versa. Although these words are closely related, often going hand-in-hand, Tolkien's intentional choice of words is significant. Pity and mercy ought to be considered as distinct words because Tolkien uses them distinctly. The difference between pity and mercy is that pity — or empathy — sees people hurting and chooses to feel their pain, but mercy responds. Mercy requires action, or often, the withholding of a deserved action.

Gollum's story is brimming with examples of both pity and mercy. Furthermore, *The Lord of the Rings* as a whole is rich with both straightforward and nuanced examples of these concepts that reinforce their importance to Tolkien and his readers alike.

The Gollum Lens
When we are first invited into Middle-earth through *The Hobbit*, we read the story of Bilbo's encounter with Gollum. In this scene, Bilbo fully expects to be killed by Gollum, but, in a game of riddles, Bilbo escapes with both his life and Gollum's Precious Ring. The Ring, of course, makes him invisible; the tables have turned, and now it is Gollum's death that seems certain. However, Gollum's defenselessness and desperation stir up pity in Bilbo. The mere sight of the helpless creature prompts Bilbo to choose pity, and, mercifully, he cannot bring himself to strike (*H* 133). This story introduces readers to the way Tolkien values pity and mercy and immediately links these concepts with the story of Gollum.

Years later, as Gandalf reveals the Ring's background to Frodo, this story comes up again. Perhaps more adamantly than any character, Gandalf acknowledges the fact that Gollum "deserve[s] death," and yet he pities the depraved creature and advocates for a merciful response to his pain and suffering (*LotR* I.2.59). Frodo initially rejects this perspective, but Gandalf's words seem to prompt a distinct shift in Frodo's perception of Gollum. This interaction has a profound impact on Frodo — and on the outcome of the Quest.

Despite hearing from Gandalf that Gollum may be "bound up with the fate of the Ring," Frodo does not feel pity or act mercifully merely because he selfishly expects Gollum to help him complete the Quest (*LotR* I.2.59). Although it may seem that Frodo is not entirely selfless in his dealings with Gollum, his treatment of him consistently models pity and mercy. Much of this empathy stems from the identity of Ring-bearer that he shares with Gollum (Waito 170). Frodo understands the inherent dangers of carrying the Ring; he has been tempted and tortured by it and has felt its power negatively impact him. He knows the suffering and turmoil that Gollum likely faced as bearer of the One Ring. Frodo may not be able to match Gollum's five-hundred-plus years in the Ring-bearer role, but he can certainly empathize with the painful burden of possessing the Ring (Arthur 20).[75] He understands the nature of Gollum's corruption since he currently bears the temptation of the same corrupting force. Gollum is a poignant reminder of the strife he experiences himself, and Frodo chooses to empathize with this fellow Ring-bearer.

After learning Gollum's history and gradually becoming aware of his presence at their heels, Sam and Frodo finally meet him face-to-face (*LotR* IV.1.614). Gollum's reputation for evil is immediately reinforced as he attacks Sam and bites his shoulder. Instinctively, Frodo threatens to kill him, and Gollum recoils in fear. Angrily nursing his wound, Sam suggests tying Gollum up and leaving him to die, but Frodo changes his mind about killing Gollum and refuses this cruelty. Frodo then recalls his previous conversation with Gandalf back in the Shire and lowers his sword, saying, "[N]ow that I see him, I do pity him" (*LotR* IV.1.615). By pausing to really see Gollum, Frodo is able to extend pity.

Gollum has not only endangered their Quest but has also injured Sam, so Frodo decides to hold him captive instead of allowing him to roam freely. However, this response is not devoid of mercy. Frodo stares directly into Gollum's eyes and explains the bargain: if Gollum agrees to guide them to Mordor, they will take a significant risk by leaving him unbound and unharmed (*LotR* IV.1.615–16). This deliberate gaze is what first prompts Frodo's use of Gollum's given name: Sméagol. In this moment, Frodo makes a commitment to recognize Gollum's dignity even in the midst of his corruption. When Frodo truly takes the time to see Gollum, choosing pity becomes natural. And all of this pity culminates in risky mercy.

---

[75] Readers may wonder why it is that Gollum's extensive possession of the Ring does not corrupt him into a more villainous presence. Although he was under the influence of the Ring for so many years, he neither joins forces with Sauron nor makes any effort to grasp at global power or domination. A likely answer to this question can be seen in the fact that throughout both *The Hobbit* and *The Lord of the Rings*, the One Ring corrupts its bearers by amplifying their individual natures. This phenomenon is perhaps best illustrated by the fact that in the single moment when Sam considers bearing the Ring, he imagines using it not to destroy or dominate but merely to make the world a garden (*LotR* VI.1.901). While the Ring would have been profoundly dangerous in the hands of powerful leaders such as Gandalf or Galadriel, it merely augments Gollum's mischievous nature and desire to have his basic needs met. Of course, the Ring corrupts these into something so powerful that they cause Gollum to lie, sneak, cheat, and kill, but ultimately, he is drawn by the power of the Ring to fulfill his simple — and sometimes petty — needs.

That night, Gollum once again proves to be unreliable. He jumps on Frodo and Sam in their false sleep, which seems to leave them no choice but to bind his ankle with Sam's rope (*LotR* IV.1.617). This elven rope causes Gollum to writhe in pain, and Gollum earnestly begs them to take it off. At first, Frodo declines. But then, "he pause[s] a moment in thought" before saying that he will consider untying the rope if Gollum can make a trustworthy promise to behave (*LotR* IV.1.618). This pause gives Frodo a moment to orient himself toward pity, which prompts him to act mercifully. Although punishment would be justly deserved, Frodo risks trusting Gollum again, binding him with a promise instead of a rope (*LotR* IV.1.618). Frodo justly keeps Gollum captive but never denies him empathy.

Frodo provides another particularly powerful example of the risk involved in mercy at the forbidden pool of Henneth Annûn. Faramir brings Frodo and Sam to a ledge overlooking the great pool where a dark figure fishes below. Driven to fulfill justice, Faramir is tempted to bid his archers to shoot, but he first turns to Frodo to ask his advice. Frodo realizes that the mysterious figure is Gollum and begs Faramir not to kill him. Then, Frodo acts in an astonishingly merciful way by risking himself for Gollum's sake. He gives Faramir's men permission to shoot him instead of Gollum if he fails to bring him back to the group, sacrificing himself for the vile creature (*LotR* IV.6.684–86).

Frodo then climbs down to Gollum's fishing spot, taking a substantial risk for Gollum, who continues to be irksome. Once again, Frodo proves his commitment to acknowledge Gollum's dignity, evidenced here by his use of the name Sméagol (*LotR* IV.6.687). Frodo's repeated choice to empathize with and show mercy to Gollum regardless of what results is monumental. His generous extension of mercy toward Gollum exemplifies commitment to pay attention to and care for others, despite the immense risks this entails.

On the other hand, Samwise Gamgee takes more than 900 pages to finally extend pity or mercy to Gollum. Throughout the Quest, Sam attacks Gollum (*LotR* IV.1.614), has to restrain murderous thoughts about him (*LotR* IV.2.623), severely distrusts him (*LotR* IV.3.638), manipulates him (*LotR* IV.4.651–54), calls him a villain to his face (*LotR* IV.8.714), and strongly desires to kill him (*LotR* IV.9.726). When it comes to the way he treats Gollum for most of the story, Sam is far from merciful. Even pity seems impossible. Despite Frodo's continued pity and mercy toward Gollum, Sam maintains a stubborn loathing throughout most of the narrative. Since Sam is so devoted to his master, this presents him with a dilemma.[76] He must wrestle with the tension between obedience to his master's wishes and what he deems just and safe.

As mentioned earlier, pity requires slowness and intentionality, preventing people from succumbing to their immediate impulses and snap judgments. Throughout the entire Quest, Sam grapples with rash thoughts about vengeance and murder, but in the end, when Sam has Gollum all to himself, his thought process slows. In the heart of Mount Doom, Gollum grovels at Sam's feet, begging for compassion. Here, at the climax, when Sam finally has the chance he has been waiting for, he wavers. He slows down just enough to be affected by pity and finds that he cannot bring himself to end Gollum's life. Although he is convinced that killing Gollum would not only be the safe option but would also be fully just and deserved, something about the "shrivelled" creature finally strikes an empathetic chord in his heart (*LotR* VI.3.944). Sam stumbles over his pardoning words, throwing jumbled insults at Gollum as he pushes him away (*LotR* VI.3.944).

It is this final, pity-prompted act of mercy that achieves the Quest (Hammond and Scull 616). Gollum slinks away from Sam but turns back to Frodo shortly after, drawn by the fierce temptation of the Ring. Then, all at once, but almost as if in slow motion, Frodo chooses not to destroy the Ring, Gollum strikes Sam, Frodo puts the Ring on, Gollum attacks the invisible Frodo and bites off his Ring finger, and Gollum falls into the fiery core of Mount Doom, destroying himself and the Ring simultaneously (*LotR* VI.3.945–46). Pure mercy is at work here: Gollum has given no indication of repentance, and, despite Gandalf's initial hunch about Gollum's part to play in the destruction of the Ring, Sam could not have predicted the fortunate triumph achieved by Gollum's final act. It is through good fortune, not any sort of wise foresight from Sam, that pity and mercy bring about good ends.[77] Although Gollum becomes the final player in the fulfillment of the Quest, the pity, mercy, and self-restraint of Frodo and Sam — as well as that of Bilbo, Gandalf, and Faramir — are what ultimately bring about the destruction of the Ring.

---

[76] This master-servant dynamic between Frodo and Sam is explored more extensively by Bunnel's section entitled "Relationships of Complement" in Ch. 3.

[77] David Bratman's distillation of this idea has significantly augmented this chapter.

Broadening the Scope

Tolkien weaves pity and mercy throughout parts of the narrative far beyond Gollum's story. The way Théoden responds to the question of what to do with Gríma the Wormtongue demonstrates a quiet instance of pity that speaks volumes. When Théoden calls all his men to be ready to ride to battle, Wormtongue offers to stay back at the Golden Hall to protect Théoden and his treasure. In response, Wormtongue is challenged to ride into battle as well. His counterfeit selflessness crumbles, and his evil intentions are exposed as he falls to the ground, anxiously pleading for both pity and mercy (*LotR* III.6.519).

Éomer, one of the commanding Marshals of Rohan, draws his sword to punish Wormtongue for his selfishness, but just as pity "stayed" Bilbo's sword-grasping hand when he considered killing Gollum many decades prior, Gandalf restrains Éomer's sword-grasping hand (*LotR* I.2.59; III.6.520). Gandalf admits matter-of-factly that killing Wormtongue would be a perfectly just decision, but he also gently reminds Éomer and Théoden of Wormtongue's humanity. He acknowledges that, although Wormtongue has fallen from what he once was, this does not mean he ought to be served death. Théoden chooses to open himself to pity and then extends mercy, freeing Wormtongue to make his own choice between service to the good and pursuit of his own desires (*LotR* III.6.520).[78]

This particular instance of pity-turned-mercy includes a curious twist: Wormtongue asks for it. Readers may wonder how the scene would have played out if Wormtongue had not begged for mercy or whether the impact of mercy is somehow lessened when it is requested. At first glance, the fact that Théoden concedes to a desperate plea can make his expression of mercy seem insincere or incomplete. However, Théoden's response to Wormtongue's petition actually demonstrates a mercy deeper than it initially seems.

Certainly, Wormtongue seeks personal safety by begging to remain at the Golden Hall, demonstrating the twisted motivation embedded in this request. In asking to stay back to protect Théoden, he tries to conceal not only selfishness but also ill intent. Gandalf unearths Wormtongue's treachery, explaining that he plans to hurt rather than heal Théoden (*LotR* III.6.521). The king recognizes

---

[78] Jung explores this scene through the lens of restoration in his section "Leaders as Redeemers" in Ch. 4.

Wormtongue's request as deceitful, which provides a reasonably founded justification to kill him, as he poses a legitimate threat. Yet, even so, Théoden — moved by pity and by Gandalf — takes a risk by releasing his hold on justice and agreeing to let Wormtongue go free. There is no hidden motive or promise that this mercy will come back to benefit Théoden, and yet Théoden chooses mercy anyway. Whereas Wormtongue only asks for his life, Théoden grants him life, freedom, and the horse that allows him to find it (*LotR* III.6.521). Théoden's risky mercy is a testament to the compelling force of pity.

Pity and mercy are also demonstrated when Gandalf and Pippin arrive at Minas Tirith. They encounter Beregond, a soldier of Gondor, who is asked to inform Pippin about the city since he is off watch duty at the time (*LotR* V.1.760). His guard shift comes later, during the Battle of the Pelennor Fields. During the battle, Pippin alerts him to Denethor's impending attempt to commit suicide and murder Faramir. Beregond must "choose between orders and the life of Faramir" (*LotR* V.4.827). He chooses to put Faramir before his job, leaving the guard post in hopes of saving Faramir from his father (*LotR* V.7.851–54). Beregond puts both his job and his life at risk by choosing to disobey orders — a daring act of mercy. The reader does not have access to Beregond's thoughts leading up to this decision, but, based on what we know about the risk involved in extending mercy, we can imagine that pity may play a role in this choice.

In Denethor's final moments, Gandalf shares with him the same thing he taught Frodo in Book I: finite beings do not have the power to grant life and, therefore, must not determine death either (*LotR* V.7.853). Furious, Denethor raises his knife and rushes toward Faramir, but, before he can strike the fatal blow, Beregond resolutely plants himself between Denethor and his son (*LotR* V.7.854). Beregond does not hesitate to risk himself for Faramir, modeling the courage involved in mercy.

Although abandoning his post is traitorous from Gondor's perspective, Beregond's risky act is met with Aragorn's mercy at the end of the book. When Aragorn rises to the throne and summons Beregond to appear before him, he calmly reminds Beregond that the traditional punishment for a guard leaving his watch post is death. Yet Aragorn excuses Beregond from this death penalty, citing Beregond's bravery in battle and sacrificial love for Faramir. Aragorn masterfully enacts justice and mercy at the same time, maintaining righteousness and lawfulness while still bestowing rewards for

Beregond's honorable and risky actions. He removes Beregond from the Guard of the Citadel and sends him out of Minas Tirith — a justly deserved consequence — only to assign him to be the captain of the White Company, otherwise known as the Guard of Faramir — an astonishing honor (*LotR* VI.5.968–69).

The Risky Choice
We can learn a great deal from revisiting *The Lord of the Rings*, particularly as we attend to the many expressions of pity and mercy. Equating pity with empathy emphasizes the value of putting ourselves in others' shoes. When Frodo relates himself to Gollum as a fellow Ring-bearer, mercy flows naturally (Waito 170). Understanding that "he himself might have met the same fate" softens Frodo's heart toward Gollum (Rutledge 58).

Taking this empathetic posture naturally prompts merciful responses to the pain of those around us. One way to practice mercy is to be sensitive in the way we name others. At the stairs of Cirith Ungol, Gollum watches Sam and Frodo sleep peacefully, and the reader watches Gollum gingerly approach Frodo. This moment has turning-point-like potential, as Gollum touches Frodo's knee in an almost "caress" (*LotR* IV.8.714). At that very moment, Sam awakens and immediately classifies this touch as dangerous. Sam questions Gollum's behavior, hastily labeling it as "sneaking" (*LotR* IV.8.714). In a flash, Gollum withdraws, destroying the redemptive potential of the scene (*LotR* IV.8.715). When Frodo rises and addresses him by the name of Sméagol, Gollum responds by calling himself a sneak. Frodo chides him for identifying himself negatively, to which Gollum answers that Master Samwise gave him that title first (*LotR* IV.8.715). He has taken Sam's harsh, judgmental words to heart.

The argument can be made that Sam's merciless treatment at this critical moment stifles any further possibility that Gollum can be redeemed. Up to this point in the text, readers receive glimpses of Gollum's real identity as Sméagol, and these glimpses keep the hope of his redemption alive. But, after this scene, no more glimmers of hope appear. Some scholars argue that Sam's harsh naming "drives [Gollum's] capacity for goodness away" entirely (Stoddard 11). Others believe that Gollum was on the verge of repentance and that "Sam waking up spoiled his chance" (Bramlett 21). This idea contradicts the typical perception of Sam as loving and heroic, demonstrating that words have tremendous power and that even the kindest characters can cause irreparable harm if they do not allow pity and mercy to drive them.

On the other hand, Frodo's commitment to use the name Sméagol demonstrates that despite this character's wretched and miserable history, Frodo still sees him for who he really is: a fellow hobbit. Whereas hasty labels demean and humiliate, true names honor deeply rooted identity.[79]

Bilbo, Gandalf, Frodo, Faramir, and eventually Sam all meet Gollum's repulsiveness with surprising pity and mercy at some point throughout his life. Théoden grants Wormtongue's plea not to be called into battle, even though freeing Wormtongue puts himself at risk. Beregond puts his position and his life on the line for the sake of Faramir, despite the fact that deserting his guard duties guarantees severe punishment. Aragorn justly disciplines Beregond for this action, but he also rewards his risky mercy with great honor. These scenes all illustrate the startling nature of pity and mercy.

Perhaps most startling of all is the fact that pity and mercy are the salvation of both Middle-earth and Frodo himself, even if they do not save Gollum (*Letters* 234, 252). Had Gollum not been shown pity and mercy numerous times throughout his life, he would not have been present at the peak of Mount Doom to keep Frodo from escaping with the Ring. And even though Frodo's mercy never guarantees him any personal benefit, in the end it provides him freedom from the burden of the Ring forever. This personal salvation is reflected on a global scale: Middle-earth is preserved indirectly because of pity and mercy.

The fact that Gollum is not redeemed but is still instrumental in the salvation of Middle-earth is profound. It reminds us that there is real danger in taking the fates of others into our own hands, for we cannot predict the future. Time and time again, the quests of our world will be completed in unpredictable ways. And if we posture ourselves so as to cultivate pity and extend mercy, we allow the opportunity for good to unfold.

---

[79] For another analysis of true names, see Harbman's section "Enchantment in Middle-earth" in Ch. 8.

Chapter 7

Providence at Work
Jacob Bradley

Sam and Frodo's escape from Mount Doom is not only one of the most powerful moments in *The Lord of the Rings* but is also one of the most controversial. The improbable rescue by the eagles prompts many questions, causing some to wonder why the eagles did not simply fly the hobbits to Mordor in the first place. Even fans of Tolkien are split between deciding if their timely arrival is more of a mistake than a miracle (Massa). This development in the story likely comes as a surprise to readers, but for Bilbo or Gandalf, this would not seem out of place. They are both helped by the eagles at some point.[80] Those who have previously witnessed the eagles intervening for the sake of what is good in Middle-earth are likely to experience hope and joy when they see the signs of their return.

Whether this winged rescue is viewed as positive or negative, there is a tendency for readers to rationalize it as mere coincidence. Popular adaptations of Tolkien's work often attribute the characters' success solely to their own heroism, undermining other factors at work. While the actions of heroes such as Aragorn, Treebeard, or Sam certainly contribute to the success of the Fellowship's Quest, their efforts are only partially responsible for the victory of the Free Peoples in Middle-earth. Nearly every character that fights for good is at one point saved from evils by something outside of his or her control. On their own, these events could quickly be written off as luck or coincidence. However, something other than random chance is at work. There appears to be more purpose behind the turn of events than luck would suggest. A closer look at the text hints that the good perseveres in Middle-earth at every turn because of providence.

We can begin to understand providence in Middle-earth by looking at Tolkien's reflections on providence in his own life. Tolkien

---

[80] For a more detailed explanation and argument for the eagles' involvement in the affairs of Middle-earth, see LaSala "In Defense of Tolkien's *Deus Ex Machina*."

often wrote to his son Christopher while he was away in the British Royal Air Force. He regularly shared parental advice along with manuscripts of the latest chapters of *The Lord of the Rings* as he was writing it. In a letter written during the Second World War, Tolkien discusses all the evil in world events, but acknowledges that "evil labours with vast power and perpetual success — in vain: preparing always only the soil for unexpected good to sprout in" (*Letters* 76). Tolkien observes a pattern of good triumphing over evil that is more than the result of luck or chance; it is indicative of divine providence coordinating seemingly disconnected events toward a certain end. While this guidance can manifest in many different forms, it always leaves room for unexpected good.

Moments of Foresight

Normally, knowledge is gained through observation or by receiving information from those who have direct experience themselves. However, several instances in *The Lord of the Rings* involve characters knowing things that neither they nor anyone else present could have witnessed, pointing to an unseen actor who is revealing that information to them. These moments of foresight — including premonitions, prophecies, visions, and dreams — suggest the intervention of a higher power in Middle-earth. Such a connection is evident in Tolkien's influences — Catholicism and various myths — which explicitly connect supernatural foresight to the activity of divine providence. Although there are many examples of foresight in this tale, two important aspects of the role of providence in the world are exemplified by Boromir's dream and the visions from Galadriel's Mirror.[81]

Boromir is inspired to go to Rivendell because of a recurring dream that he and his brother Faramir both receive. In this dream, a vision of darkness in the East is met by a light in the West that speaks a prophetic poem about a broken sword that must be found (*LotR* II.2.246). The dream shows the growing threat of Sauron from Mordor and a response from the West. This is significant because the West is the home of the Valar, the angel-like beings who govern Middle-earth. The Valar are reaching out through this dream — first to Faramir and later

---

[81] Aragorn also has several recorded instances of foresight where his premonitions are later confirmed, such as when he meets Éomer on the Pelennor Fields (*LotR* V.6.848).

to Boromir — to give them the information they need to help destroy the evil of the Ring and Sauron. The repetition of the dreams as well as the foresight they provide indicate the divine origins of the message.

Other accounts of visions in the book have less explicit origins but focus more on how the receivers respond to them, such as those granted by the Mirror of Galadriel. Through her use of elven-magic, the Mirror reveals visions of the past, present, and what might be (*LotR* II.7.362). Perhaps she learned this art from associating with divine beings in ages past, but Tolkien leaves its exact origin a mystery. However, as scholar David C. Powell comments, even though Galadriel speaks "with a measure of truth, [...] the knowledge is only as accurate as her perception skills permit" (44). The visions mix up events in a way that makes causality unclear to the viewer, and, therefore, they are not always helpful (*LotR* II.7.363). Elves are not always able to interpret these visions correctly. However, this does not diminish their ability to influence the future by acting in response to visions about it.

In *The Lord of the Rings*, providence allows for the operation of people's free will to play a part in shaping the fate of the world. In this, Tolkien may be borrowing from the Anglo-Saxons. The Anglo-Saxon King Alfred explains in his version of Boethius's *Consolation of Philosophy* — an important source for Tolkien — that "fate" roughly equates to "consequences of decisions" (Deyo 61).[82] Fate is not set in stone until it has actually happened. Although the outcome of history is known to God, our choices are still free. Likewise, the prophetic visions from the Mirror show that future events can be altered or brought about by the onlookers' actions, although the exact effects of their actions are unknown until they occur. Galadriel holds this view: after Frodo resolves to take the Ring to Mordor, she tells the hobbits that "now we have chosen, and the tides of fate are flowing" (*LotR* III.7.336). The beauty of providence is that it not only accounts for all individual choices (good and bad) in its design, but also that it is by those independent choices that history moves toward its directed path.

Therefore, as Tolkien scholar Kathleen E. Dubs writes, "free will operates within the order of the universe [providence], fate being merely the earthly manifestation of that order" (40). While Boromir's dream might tempt the reader to believe that his actions

---

[82] This is, of course, no surprise to the designs of providence in the Anglo-Saxon view.

were controlled by the prodding of an intervening power, the episode at Galadriel's Mirror makes it clear that foreknowledge of future events does not rob us of the power of choice in making a meaningful difference. We may still choose to do good or not, as fate is a response to actions and not the other way around.

Tolkien uses moments of foresight like these in his story to remind the reader that his characters' fates are not as random as they may seem. Rather, they are informed by and dependent on the action of an unseen intervening power. Although the idea of an individual being moved towards good action through revelation or foresight may seem a matter of pure fantasy, it is not unheard of for one's intuition to bring about an unexpected good. For example, it may be providential that someone with an unprompted desire to call a friend then happens to find out their friend is in a time of dire need. Or a dream may cause someone to think through a potential course of events that they then seek to avoid or bring about in their life. Some may approach these things with a natural amount of skepticism, but most are willing to admit that they have benefitted on some occasion by an unexplained or supernatural feeling.

Meetings of Chance
One of the earliest indications of providence at work in the story is when Gandalf explains the Ring's journey from Sauron's hand to Frodo's. The long and fortuitous path it takes from one intermediary to the next demonstrates that "Bilbo was *meant* to find the Ring," and that this did not happen by any plans of either Sauron or Bilbo (*LotR* I.2.56). According to theologian Fleming Rutledge, Gandalf's explanation indicates the presence of "something else at work" (*LotR* I.2.56) beyond both Ring-maker and Ring-bearer (Rutledge 62). While Gandalf may not name exactly who this actor is, it is clear that this pattern of chance encounters with the Ring eventually sets the events that lead to the defeat of evil in Middle-earth in motion. This hints that casual meetings are not always mere happenstance.

On a first read, it appears that Frodo and his companions are assisted by a fair number of chance meetings. The first villain the hobbits face in their long journey is not an orc or a wraith but a tree named Old Man Willow. During the hobbits' trek through the Old Forest, Old Man Willow attempts to kill them by swallowing Merry and Pippin and drowning Frodo in the creek. Fortunately, Tom Bombadil is there to save them. When asked, he claims to have come their way by chance, "if chance you call it" (*LotR* I.7.126). Because of that meeting, he also helps them later when they are trapped by the Barrow-wights. It is easy to dismiss the crossing of their paths as simply a *deus ex machina*. However, the continued use of the term "chance" by other characters suggests a greater significance than just convenience for the author.

At face value, it is odd that the characters who form the Fellowship are all at Rivendell, especially considering that Elrond did not call them there. Elrond even uses the word "chance" to describe their first meeting. Upon gathering the council, he tells the party that they are "called" to this meeting by what seems to be "chance," but really because "it is so ordered" that they would have the task of deciding what to do with the Ring laid upon them (*LotR* II.2.243). It is clear to Elrond that the crossing of their paths is anything but coincidence. Tolkien scholar Rogery Drury notes that even though the agent behind this "chance" meeting is left anonymous, Elrond "indicates that this agent is willful, it does order varied elements, and it is trying to aid the Council's endeavors" (8). In other words, each member of the party comes to Rivendell of his own will, but they all remain unified in their cause by some power enacting its will in Middle-earth.

Readers have good reason to trust Elrond's judgment that this meeting is more than chance. Numbered among the Wise, Elrond has lived through many ages of Middle-earth and thus has a more experienced view of the world.[83] He is particularly fond of speaking in terms of fate, like many of his kin from *The Silmarillion*, where he and Galadriel, among others, are more directly involved in divine affairs. In *The Lord of the Rings*, long-lived characters such as Gandalf, Bombadil, Elrond, and Galadriel tend to have greater foresight and use terms such as fate or chance more openly in their speech than the shorter-lived races of Dwarves, Men, or Hobbits. This is because the Wise have witnessed a pattern of providential design through ages of experience with it. As Peter Kreeft points out, "You can see the hand of providence more clearly if you become more familiar with it, like the face of a stranger who becomes a friend" (58). Returning readers will, like the Wise, begin to see providence's influence more clearly.

---

[83] In *The Lord of the Rings*, "the Wise" chiefly refers to the group of Wizards and Elf leaders who meet as members of the White Council to oppose Sauron (*LotR* App.B.1085).

When readers begin to look for them, there are plenty of examples of providence bringing people together through chance meetings. When Frodo and Sam are in danger of being detected by the Enemy as they approach Mordor, they are captured by Faramir. Although Sam fears that all is lost when he accidentally reveals to this stranger that Frodo holds the One Ring, Faramir tells him that "it was fated to be so" and that all will go well (*LotR* IV.5.681). Their meeting turns out to be fortunate because Faramir gives the two hobbits protection and supplies them with the means to continue their journey to Mount Doom. Just when Frodo and Sam unexpectedly find themselves at the mercy of another, it turns out that this person is honest and trustworthy. When these favorable meetings of chance continue throughout the story, the guidance of providence in world events seems more credible than coincidence. In the end, the members of the Fellowship find themselves at the right places at just the right times far more often than mere chance can explain.

Convergence of Events
The way that seemingly independent events converge provides further evidence of providence at work in the story. The Fellowship often benefits from the fortunate timing of others' actions that impact their Quest, despite great distance and lack of communication. For example, Faramir believes Sam and Frodo's story of traveling with his brother Boromir because less than two weeks before, an unusual light on the water led Faramir to find his brother's horn drifting on the same boat that carried him down the Falls of Rauros (*LotR* IV.5.666). One week's difference and the hobbits could have been received very differently in Ithilien. Aragorn, Gimli, and Legolas did not know what would happen as a result of their choosing to send the boat with Boromir's body down the river, but the fact that this choice saves Frodo and Sam later on indicates either a great amount of luck or an act of providence.

Another such example is when Frodo fortunately avoids the fatal mistake of revealing himself to Sauron on the summit of Amon Hen. Frodo experiences visions across the lands of Middle-earth until he gazes upon Mordor and the Eye of Sauron rests upon him (*LotR* II.10.401). However, he becomes aware of another will — later revealed to be Gandalf — that releases him from Sauron's grasp for an instant to freely choose whether to give in to the Shadow or accept the burden of the Quest (*LotR* II.10.401). This episode demonstrates the incredible timing of

Frodo's rescue, as he is saved from the grasp of the Enemy only because Gandalf happens at that moment to be at a high place from which he can contend with Sauron's will (*LotR* III.5.495). As a result, this unforeseen encounter saves Frodo from certain disaster at the hands of the Enemy.

Sam and Frodo are not the only hobbits to benefit from a series of uncoordinated events that seem to align in their favor. When Merry and Pippin are kidnapped by the Uruks, Grishnákh tries to kill the helpless hobbits but is struck down by the arrow of a Rohirrim ambusher "aimed with skill, or guided by fate" (*LotR* III.3.457). The night raid by the Riders of Rohan allows the hobbits to escape into Fangorn Forest where they meet Treebeard. Gandalf later tells Aragorn and his companions that the hobbits coming to Fangorn Forest "was like the falling of small stones that starts an avalanche in the mountains" (*LotR* III.5.496). Because Merry and Pippin are introduced to their Ent hosts, the armies of Isengard are defeated at Helm's Deep by the Ents and the Huorns. Isengard is also besieged at the perfect time, when the hosts of Saruman's Uruk-hai have left and the fortress is assailable.

Without these seemingly unrelated events coming together in full convergence, Isengard would never have been overthrown, the Quest would never have been fulfilled, and the Ring would never have been destroyed. Perhaps uncoordinated events are more related than they initially appear. Providence has the power to bring together these events into one cohesive story.

Unexpectedly Useful Objects

Providence in Middle-earth also has a way of placing both ordinary and extraordinary objects in just the right hands.[84] Many of the unexpectedly useful objects in *The Lord of the Rings* are gifts given to the Fellowship along their journey. They are largely forgotten until characters are placed in situations where these items become crucial to victory over unforeseen challenges. Although there are many items of special significance that could be mentioned, the gifts that Galadriel gives to Pippin, Frodo, Merry, and Sam, respectively, are perhaps the most instrumental in the completion of the Quest.

After Pippin and Merry are taken as prisoners by the Uruk-hai, it is the elven brooch that Pippin receives in Lothlórien that helps Aragorn,

---

[84] See Mar's section on "Ordinary Objects" in Ch. 2 for a more thorough analysis of this idea.

Legolas, and Gimli to stay on the hobbits' trail and reunite with Gandalf. The brooch becomes surprisingly useful when Pippin drops it to mark his trail; it is small enough not to be noticed by their captors yet distinct enough to be recognized by his companions who are following him.[85] It remains something of a miracle that an object of that size is noticed when it could have been anywhere along the path of their three-day-long hunt, with no hint that they should expect to look for it.

This is not the only surprising use of an object that the Fellowship receives from Galadriel. After remaining forgotten for the majority of Frodo and Sam's journey, the phial that Galadriel gives Frodo becomes essential to completing the Quest. The phial, which shines with a light like the stars, seems like an impractical gift for someone who is trying to sneak past their enemy. Until reaching the stairs that lead to Shelob's lair, Frodo has refrained from using it out of fear of being exposed by its light (*LotR* IV.9.720). However, Frodo fortunately gives the phial to Sam in the tunnels of Cirith Ungol. Emboldened by the light of the phial, Sam regains his courage and wards off Shelob against all odds (*LotR* IV.10.729–30). The phial also allows Sam to overcome the malice of the Watchers at the Gate of Cirith Ungol and defeat them once more when he leaves with Frodo (*LotR* VI.1.902, 915).[86] Not only is the phial more useful than expected, it is also more useful to Sam than to Frodo, its intended bearer.

Merry's sword is also an object that finds better use in the hands of someone other than its original owner. Tom Bombadil gives Merry the sword from the treasure hoard of the Barrow-wights, who protected the grave of an ancient Dúnedain king of Arnor (*LotR* I.8.145). Unknown to the hobbits, this blade was made specifically to destroy the Nazgûl many years ago when the northern kingdoms warred with the power of the Witch-king of Angmar, the very same being who now leads Sauron's armies against Gondor and is said to be unkillable by any man (*LotR* App.A.I.4.1051). In the hands of a hobbit, this specially enchanted blade helps defeat the Witch-king by dispelling

---

[85] The cloaks fastened with the brooches first enter the possession of the company in Lothlórien on 15 Feb. (*LotR* II.5.370). Pippin lets his brooch go on 27 Feb. (*LotR* III.3.450). Legolas finds it on 1 Mar. (*LotR* III.2.424).

[86] Interestingly, the phial of Galadriel does not provide light for Sam on Mount Doom (*LotR* VI.3.945). This is possibly because Tolkien describes Sam as being fearful and uncertain at this moment, whereas he had exhibited courage in prior instances when the phial was activated in his hands.

the magic that holds him together and weakening him enough so that Éowyn, the shieldmaiden of Rohan, can kill the evil creature (*LotR* V.6.842). Merry does not know that the weapon he holds is the only thing capable of weakening the Witch-king, nor did he plan to meet the leader of the Nazgûl on his journey, but somehow these unrelated events become connected in the grand scheme of things.

One might argue that this evidence of providence is nothing more than the work of an author who weaves the plot of his story seamlessly from earlier scenes into others. But an author as thorough in his world-building as Tolkien would only do this because it is consistent with his overall conception of Middle-earth — one in which providence is not limited by time as it integrates events both past and present to bring about future good.

The unexpected impact of certain objects is especially evident when Sam uses a box of earth from Lothlórien to rebuild the Shire when he returns home. Galadriel gives Sam a small quantity of dirt for use in his personal garden (*LotR* II.5.375). He cherishes this box during the whole journey, at one point choosing to keep it even over his beloved pots and pans. This proves to be beneficial. When they return to the Shire, the hobbits find it ransacked and desolated by the tyrant Sharkey and his ruffians who have burned or uprooted most of the trees of their homeland. After the four hobbits rally their countrymen and expel the invaders, Sam uses the dirt not only to grow his own garden but to restore abundance to all the land of the Shire, which had become a treeless wasteland. Goodness coming out of a small box of dirt once again hints at the presence of the supernatural.

Culmination at Mount Doom

Perhaps the greatest evidence of providence at work in *The Lord of the Rings* revolves around Gollum because his involvement in the story incorporates chance meetings, moments of foresight, converging events, and unexpectedly useful objects. It is an accidental encounter with orcs in the mountains that leads Bilbo to meet Gollum and consequently find the Ring, and it is his choice to spare Gollum that unforeseeably results in the success of Frodo's mission years later (*LotR* Prologue.4.11). Before the Quest even begins, Gandalf predicts that Gollum "has some part to play yet, for good or ill, before the end" (*LotR* I.2.59). Even the moment when Frodo gives in to the temptation of the Ring and takes it for himself is an example of providence.

Frodo has persevered for so long without giving in to the evil around his neck that by the time he does, he is just weak enough for Gollum to overpower him. Tolkien writes in a letter that "Frodo had done what he could and spent himself completely (as an instrument of Providence) and had produced a situation in which the object of his quest could be achieved" (*Letters* 326). Ironically, the Ring prompts both Frodo's enfeeblement and Gollum's aggression. By corrupting both Frodo and Gollum, the Ring becomes unexpectedly useful in its own destruction. The evil desire it creates in them undermines its own chances of survival by causing them to recklessly fight over it at Mount Doom. Gollum's fixation on the Ring prompts him to "gloat on his prize" after stealing it from Frodo, taking a step too far backwards, falling off the edge and destroying the Ring and Sauron (*LotR* VI.3.946). This accurately depicts how providence works in Middle-earth — not through isolated events but through the harmonizing of all elements, both good and bad, throughout time to craft a good ending.

Bringing It Home
The scope of providence in *The Lord of the Rings* is broad enough that it could make a convincing argument for a similar coordinating power in our own lives. A story that intricately weaves every detail together as if each thread were directed towards a common end strongly suggests authorial intent behind its message.[87] As the coordinating work of providence in *The Lord of the Rings* suggests, everyday occurrences can have more significance than we might think.

The Lord of the Rings reminds us that seemingly insurmountable evil can be overcome by the wills of courageous people, especially because a coordinating power greater than ourselves also wills for good to prevail. This is what Tolkien means when he writes that he thinks people, very much like the characters in his book, can "surmount" any "horror conceivable" so long as they refuse to give in to evil and allow themselves to be assisted "by grace" (*Letters* 120). In this case, the grace Tolkien refers to can manifest in different ways such as meetings of chance, moments of foresight, fortunate timing, and objects that are used in surprising ways to do good. There are also many other ways in which providence works with grace to bring

---

[87] See Kirkendall's section "Detours" in Ch. 1 for the impact of interlace on the narrative.

good out of any circumstances that are beyond human understanding. Perhaps this is why readers may feel something special after reading about the eagles coming to save the hobbits on Mount Doom. If the grace that works through providence orders the world so that creatures as small as hobbits are empowered to resist the temptation of evil, then there is cause for real hope. And that is no coincidence.

Chapter 8

An Enchanted World
Joshua Harbman

THE OPENING SCENES IN *The Lord of the Rings* give the reader plenty of time to settle into the simple rhythms of life in the Shire. A rural town buzzes with anticipation for Bilbo's impending "eleventy-first birthday" party, a momentous occasion by Hobbit standards (*LotR* I.1.21). However, even in a society as detached from the rest of the world as the Shire, murmurings of marvelous and dreadful happenings creep in (*LotR* I.2.45). These rumors of a world alive with Elves, talking trees, and dragons elicit one of two responses from Hobbits: denial or desire. This distinction is evident in a conversation between Samwise Gamgee and Ted Sandyman in the safety of a local inn, *The Green Dragon*. Sandyman, along with most of the Shire-folk, stoutly denies the existence of dragons or Tree-men. He insists that, even if the Elves are leaving Middle-earth, it will never impact daily life in the Shire (*LotR* I.2.44).

Sam, however, thinks differently. The stories Bilbo tells of the Elves produce in Sam a deep desire to experience more. He speaks, in his simple way, of his powerful longing to see Elves and Oliphaunts (*LotR* I.2.64). His yearning to encounter the world's mysteries echoes the wonder Tolkien awakens in the imagination of his readers. This openness to the unexplained aspects of the world can be termed *enchantment*.

Any world full of dragons, Elves, and talking trees might be called magical. However, it is an oversimplification to equate the overt presence of magic with the enchanted nature of Tolkien's invented world. Instead, enchantment and disenchantment are worldviews explored with nuance in Middle-earth.

A Disenchanted Wizard
Often the best way to understand something is by examining its foil. The most striking example of a disenchanted character in this magical world is Saruman. Although he is himself a wizard, Saruman

provides a frame of reference for understanding disenchantment and its consequences. His disenchantment manifests in his emphasis upon fact to the exclusion of mystery, and it results in a desire for control and an abuse of nature.

Saruman uses an ancient seeing stone, a *palantír*, to gather knowledge and, eventually, to communicate with Sauron. He believes that the extended sight of the *palantír* offers him a clear view of the state of the world. Based on what he sees there, he comes to the conclusion that Sauron is undefeatable (*LotR* II.2.259). Glimpsing the power arrayed against Middle-earth brings him to despair.[88] Saruman becomes convinced that the only option is submission to Sauron, and, looking only at the observable facts, he seems to be correct. In contrast, Elrond tells the council to take heart because there are "other powers and realms," realities beyond the *palantír* that offer hope (*LotR* II.2.267). Additionally, Gandalf encourages Frodo by assuring him that he was *"meant"* to have the Ring by some unnamed power (*LotR* I.2.56).[89] Saruman overlooks the possibility that there might be forces at work beyond his sight.

Saruman's reliance on strictly factual understanding epitomizes the disenchanted worldview. Max Weber defines disenchantment as the belief that "there are no mysterious, incalculable powers at work" in the world, and that it is possible to "master everything through calculation" (13–14).[90] Saruman holds such a worldview. Simply because he sees much, he convinces himself he can see all. His prideful dismissal of anything outside of his perspective results in a reductive and ultimately hopeless view of the world.

Saruman's desire to calculate all things leads to an obsession with control. As Saruman tries to convince Gandalf to join him, he argues that by possessing absolute power they could order all things as he thinks would be best for Middle-earth (*LotR* II.2.259). Although veiled by good intention, Saruman's desire for absolute control is a hallmark

---

[88] Denethor, the other character with consistent access to a *palantír*, goes through the same process. With the knowledge this magical tool provides, he comes to believe that there is no hope and succumbs to madness (*LotR* V.7.853).

[89] The italics are in the original, indicating Gandalf's emphasis on the presence of a benevolent force working for good. This providence is explored more fully by Bradley in Ch. 7.

[90] Max Weber is one of the earliest scholars to bring this conversation to the forefront and is still a primary source for the definitions of disenchantment and enchantment.

of the disenchanted. In *Intimations of Postmodernity*, Zygmunt Bauman writes that "the disenchantment of the world was the ideology of its subordination" (x). Saruman, unwilling to allow Middle-earth to function by itself or to content himself with the role of patient guide, attempts to demand subordination to his will. Saruman assures Gandalf that, although all sorts of evils may happen along the way, the endeavor will be worthwhile in the final pursuit of "Knowledge, Rule, [and] Order" (*LotR* II.2.259).

Saruman's disenchantment leads him to treat the natural world as nothing more than a collection of resources, an attitude which ultimately leads to his undoing. Christopher Partridge identifies this as a pattern: as the world becomes disenchanted, "nature is managed" (169). It is no longer wondrous and beloved but exploited for resources. Treebeard laments that Saruman has "a mind of metal and wheels; and he does not care for growing things, except as far as they serve him" (*LotR* III.4.473).[91] Saruman displays a disenchanted worldview by reducing the world to what is manageable and scorning any reverence for the deeper nature of things. Ironically, this ultimately incites the Ents to rise up and overthrow him.

Gandalf, on the other hand, embodies the enchanted worldview. He expects unseen forces to be working with him — and they are. While Saruman dismisses the possibility in favor of tangible information from the *palantír*, Gandalf understands that unseen forces are at work against Sauron (*LotR* I.2.56). When Gandalf is saved from Saruman's captivity by the "unlooked for" Great Eagle Gwaihir, he experiences the power of enchantment: Gandalf sees the world for what it really is, and his openness to these greater forces is what grants him unlooked for victory time and again (*LotR* II.2.261).

Moreover, Gandalf recognizes that wisdom requires seeing the world as more than the sum of its observable parts. In Gandalf's confrontation with Saruman, Saruman reveals that his obsession with mastery has caused him to turn away from his identity as Saruman the White, trusted member of The White Council. Saruman scoffs at whiteness, claiming that it is unimportant because it can be overcome

---

[91] It is not difficult to glimpse Tolkien's personal feelings in Treebeard's outrage at the way Saruman has desecrated his forest. Tolkien writes in a letter, "I am (obviously) much in love with plants and above all trees, and always have been; and I find human maltreatment of them as hard to bear as some find ill-treatment of animals" (*Letters* 220).

by dye if clothes are white, by ink if a page is white, or by a prism if the light is white (*LotR* II.2.259). In response, Gandalf sternly asserts, "he that breaks a thing to find out what it is has left the path of wisdom" (*LotR* II.2.259). Gandalf is exposing Saruman's flawed logic about the color white — just because it can be broken, does not mean that it should be or that the person who breaks it understands it more fully. Gandalf also points out the way that Saruman has abandoned his calling and accuses him of no longer being wise. In doing so, Gandalf demonstrates another hallmark of the enchanted: that things, like the color white, are more than the sum of their parts and wisdom is more than control and knowledge.

Enchantment in Middle-earth
The magic of Saruman and Gandalf, and Middle-earth generally, is distinct from the spell-casting common in fantasy worlds. In a conversation about the Elves, Sam and Frodo discuss the elusive nature of Lothlórien. Sam says that if it is magic then "it's right down deep, where I can't lay my hands on it" (*LotR* II.7.361).[92] Furthermore, the elves are taken aback when asked if their marvelous possessions are "magic" (*LotR* II.7.362). Instead, the power of the Elves cooperates with realities beyond what is observable, exactly what an enchanted worldview expects and a disenchanted worldview denies.

One example of the subtle magic of Middle-earth is the power of names. When Merry and Pippin meet Treebeard in Fangorn Forest, Treebeard is startled by the hobbits' willingness to disclose their true names (*LotR* III.4.465). Treebeard pointedly does not tell them his own. He explains that in Old Entish, names carry the story of that which they refer to (*LotR* III.4.467). In this language, names are not static. Instead, they constantly morph to better capture the changing nature of the entities they represent. However, in these latter days, many of the magical places are shrinking rather than growing, and their names shrink with them. For example, the woods of Lothlórien used to be called by a longer name, but as the forest fades, its name also diminishes (*LotR* III.4.467). In our world, we do not expect names to be intimately connected to the nature of what they refer to.

---

[92] Gerard Manley Hopkins's poem, "God's Grandeur," powerfully expresses a similar thought: "For all this nature is never spent; / There lives the dearest freshness deep down things" (14).

However, in Middle-earth, entities and their names bear an enchanted connection that alludes to a supernatural reality.

From almost the beginning of the story, characters make use of this inexplicable power of names. Before the hobbits even get out of the Shire, they get lost in the Old Forest, lulled to sleep, and are almost eaten by a nefarious old tree called Old Man Willow (*LotR* I.6.118). When all hope seems lost before the Quest has even begun, they are saved by a mysterious, singing keeper of the forest: Tom Bombadil. Bombadil runs to the tree and with only the power of his voice frees the trapped hobbits. In keeping with the depth of magic in Middle-earth, most of what Bombadil says to Old Man Willow is lost in a whisper. However, the reader clearly hears Bombadil giving commands based on the authority of his own name as he proclaims "Bombadil is talking!" (*LotR* I.6.120).

Bombadil is not the only character to do so. In his confrontation with the Balrog, Gandalf declares his identity as a "servant of the Secret Fire" (*LotR* II.5.330). Aragorn also announces his name as the Company sails the river Anduin and in the declaration seems to be changed into the likeness of the kings of old (*LotR* II.9.393).[93] These examples demonstrate a pattern: those who understand their identity draw strength from the declaration of their true names.[94]

Some characters, because they reject their identity, fail to harness this power. When Gandalf comes to Isengard, Saruman attempts to rename himself as Ring-maker and as Saruman of Many Colors (*LotR* II.2.259). Saruman's act of naming is wholly ineffective as none of this comes to fruition. Janet Brennan Croft notes that although Saruman uses these names for himself, "no one else ever does [...] because the names have little relation to the truth" (89). Saruman is not connected to either the reality of his identity or what the world is like, demonstrated perhaps most powerfully by his defeat at the limbs of the Ents.

---

[93] This also happens when Aragorn first meets Éomer (*LotR* III.2.433) and again when he defends his right to use the *palantír* (*LotR* IV.2.780). See the section "Discoveries" in Ch. 1 for the deeper significance of these declarations in light of Middle-earth's ancient history.

[94] Dickinson references the power of calling others by their true names in her section on "The Risky Choice" in Ch. 6. The power in both proclaiming one's own true name and also calling others by their names illustrates the intangible but powerful connection between a thing and its name.

The Myth of Progress

While wizards and talking trees are otherworldly examples of this dichotomy of worldviews, the same tension exists in our world. In modern culture, disenchanted thinking has become dominant (Taylor 1).[95] It is not difficult to observe the confident assumption that there are no unseen forces at work. One may explain a drought by changing weather patterns, credit an unforeseen recovery from a fatal disease to medicine or human resilience, and dismiss coincidence as mere chance.[96] This movement away from mystery and towards scientific understanding is generally viewed as unqualified progress.

The final triumph of the disenchanted worldview is the confident assertion that everything inexplicable will eventually be solved. For example, the mystery of consciousness is thought by some to be merely a neural network that someday will be perfectly understood (Zador). Although too complex to replicate with current technology, every human thought, desire, or emotion might someday be reducible to a string of ones and zeroes.

Since the Enlightenment, the assumption that civilization is opposed to enchantment has been steadily growing. As there are fewer unknowns and society progresses, disenchantment creeps in. The fringes of our maps are no longer clouded in mystery. There is no question about what is on the other side of the ocean, let alone over the next hill. This is only one example of the way progress removes uncertainty from our everyday lives. In her article "An Anthropologist in Middle-earth," Virginia Luling remarks that "in evolutionary thinking the advance of civilisation is also a progressive 'disenchantment' as people grow more rational" (55). This assumption that disenchantment represents progress is built into the modern world's default mode of thinking.

But is this a valid assumption? There are damaging consequences to this shift in thought. Peter Lowentrout argues that disenchantment has emptied the world of meaning, that "Our universe has become

---

[95] Charles Taylor begins his landmark book *A Secular Age* by saying that "Almost everyone would agree that in some sense we do [live in a secular age]." For Taylor, the rise of the secular is essentially synonymous with the disenchantment of the world that Weber describes. Taylor stipulates that by "we," he means in particular the "West" or perhaps even the "North Atlantic." This chapter maintains a similar focus on the state of culture in the West, not necessarily the rest of the world.

[96] Bradley explores the significance of seemingly coincidental events in Ch. 7.

vast, cold and objective" (47). Tolkien's work addresses this emptiness and the longing it creates.[97]

Tolkien's Worldview
Tolkien's view of the world as enchanted is clearly expressed in his poem "Mythopoeia." Tolkien's decision to express these ideas in a poem rather than an essay or lecture suggests his enchanted worldview. There would be a certain irony in defending an enchanted world through rational argument or logical proof. Tolkien is not looking merely to convince his audience, but to pull us into a profound experience that demonstrates his point. Poetry and other artistic mediums have the ability to communicate in a register that kindles emotion and imagination as well as reason.[98]

The first stanza of the poem depicts a disenchanted world, where "a star's a star, some matter in a ball / compelled to courses mathematical" ("Mythopoeia" 85).[99] These lines describe a view of the world that reduces things to only their describable, material aspects — a central tenet of the disenchanted worldview. In a world stripped of the mythical and the mysterious, all things are reducible to their component parts (Latour 115).[100]

However, Tolkien's poem suggests that this understanding does not capture the full reality of our world. "Mythopoeia" argues that claiming a star is *only* a collection of matter robs it of beauty and power. Later in the poem, Tolkien returns to this example to say that "He sees no stars who does not see them first / of living silver made that sudden burst / to flame like flowers beneath an ancient song" ("Mythopoeia" 87). Tolkien explains that long before we are old and sophisticated enough to put stars into material categories or describe them as hydrogen and helium balls, we first simply experience them as mysterious, ancient, and awe-inspiring. While stars can and should

---

[97] For an explicitly Christian and practical reflection on where the solution to the problem of longing and emptiness created by disenchantment might be found, see Cosper's *Recapturing the Wonder: Transcendent Faith in a Disenchanted World*.

[98] Because I am convinced of this, I have included footnotes to poems that convey similar content and, for me at least, carry a similar ring of truth.

[99] For another poem along a similar vein, see "When I Heard the Learn'd Astronomer" by Walt Whitman.

[100] Admittedly, some argue that the laboratory has actually been an enchanting, not a disenchanting force. As Bruno Latour puts it, "How could we be capable of disenchanting the world, when every day our laboratories and our factories populate the world with hundreds of hybrids stranger than those of the day before?" (115).

be studied scientifically, we understand their nature better when they incite wonder first.[101] We instinctively respond to the world — sunsets, mountains, and stars — with a sense of wonder. To know this, one needs only to look at a child, to whom everything is a marvel.

Viewing stars as "living silver," as Tolkien recommends, is not easily quantifiable — and that is a distinction between enchantment and disenchantment. Often, before something has been understood and accordingly diminished, it occupies a mystical space. While the disenchanted scholar looks up into a "regimented, cold, inane" universe, the enchanted observer is captivated by the beauty of a singing cosmos ("Mythopoeia" 85).[102]

Later in his poem, Tolkien warns readers about the ultimate consequences of a disenchanted worldview. Those who unquestioningly pursue progress will end up in "the dark abyss to which their progress tends / if by God's mercy progress ever ends" ("Mythopoeia" 89). Tolkien suggests that a headlong rush toward progress becomes a race to destruction. For Tolkien, the threat mechanized progress poses to the world is epitomized by "the lunatic destruction of the physical lands which Americans inhabit" (*Letters* 412). This pillaging of the land to satisfy the ever-increasing demands of new technology bears an uncomfortable similarity to Saruman's ruthless hacking of Fangorn Forest. Not only does general destruction result from a disregard of nature in favor of progress, but in the aftermath of two world wars, Tolkien remarks in a letter to his son that the "War of the Machines" has left all of humanity poorer, more bereft and with millions dead in its wake (*Letters* 111). The war ended with "only one thing triumphant: the Machines" (*Letters* 111). This bleak vision of the societal cost of progress for its own sake is a sobering reflection on the price of a disenchanted civilization.

These Dangers in Middle-earth

With an understanding of Tolkien's perspective on disenchantment, we can see how he portrays its pitfalls through the fall of the Númenóreans in *The Silmarillion*. The Númenóreans, the kingly

---

[101] Lewis addresses exactly this in *The Voyage of the Dawn Treader*: "'In our world,' said Eustace, 'a star is a huge ball of flaming gas.' 'Even in your world, [replies Ramandu] my son, that is not what a star is, but only what it is made of'" (*VDT* 226).

[102] The distinction drawn here between a disenchanted "universe" and an enchanted "cosmos" is common (Taylor 59–60; Cosper 11).

race of Men that Aragorn is distantly descended from, were blessed with knowledge handed down to them through the Valar. The great Númenórean civilization was built on an island within sight of the Blessed Realm, where the Valar dwell (*S* 260). Sauron, still clothed in light and beauty, persuades the Númenóreans to leave behind the high ideals that had defined their society. Ar-Pharazôn, their last king, presides over the moral collapse of their society as they become increasingly fixated on wealth and power. During this time, it seems to them "that they prospered, and if they were not increasing in happiness, yet they grew more strong, and their rich men even richer" (*S* 274). They develop engines and build ever more impressive ships (*S* 274). The Númenóreans mistakenly equate the increase of wealth and technology with true prosperity.

As their technology improves and wealth accumulates, they kill each other over petty grievances, and the "world [is] darkened by many a tale of dread" (*S* 274). For a long time, the Númenóreans had been envious of the immortality of the Valar but had not made any attempt to seize it for themselves. As Ar-Pharazôn feels his death approaching, he resolves to invade the Blessed Realm (*S* 275). This, he hopes, will secure for himself immortality, completing his obsession with control by even mastering death. As he sets foot in the Blessed Realm, a cataclysmic event destroys the entire invading army and sinks the island of Númenór (*S* 278–79). This swift destruction meted out upon the Númenóreans is the final result of a disenchanted desire for control.

The Númenóreans are just one example of the doomed cycle of unchecked progress. The Dwarves delve greedily and recklessly into the earth in their hunt for the precious metal *mithril*. Overcome by their desire, they mine too deep and awaken a Balrog (*LotR* App.A.III.1071–72). This primordial monster kills the Dwarves and returns Moria to darkness, showing that there is always a cost to the selfish misuse of nature (Bauman 8). Degrading the natural realm until it is merely a resource to harvest promises only catastrophe.[103]

Promise of Enchantment

While the fate of the Númenóreans and the Dwarves serve as a warning against a disenchanted pursuit of progress, Tolkien casts an

---

[103] For a thoughtful vision of an alternative way to interact with the earth that is modeled on husbandry instead of extraction, see Berry 87–105.

alternate vision of a civilization that collectively holds an enchanted worldview. Prior to the destruction brought by Ar-Pharazôn, enchantment permeated every facet of Númenórean society. The original great societies of Men depended on their interactions with the Elves. The re-establishment of civilization following the failure of Ar-Pharazôn also relies on enchantment. Elendil and his sons, who reject the lies of Sauron and escape the fall of the Númenóreans, are Aragorn's distant ancestors.

Following the destruction of their homeland, the surviving Númenóreans (also called the Dúnedain) "dwelt under the protection of the Valar and in the friendship of the Eldar, and they increased in stature both of mind and body" (*S* 261–62). They resuscitate a once great civilization only by the intervention of unfathomable forces. Elendil and his sons after him found the kingdom that becomes Gondor and "though their lore and craft was but an echo of that which had been ere Sauron came to Númenor, yet very great it seemed to the wild men of the world" (*S* 280). This underscores the fact that even the craft of civilization is not something achieved merely scientifically. Rather, it has its roots in those who maintain a belief in the enchantment of the world.

At every stage of development, the civilization of Men in Middle-earth relies on more than human ingenuity. Virginia Luling aptly points out that in Middle-earth, "civilisation and enchantment are not opposed but go together" (55). As the history of Middle-earth continues, the wondrous constantly influences the development of civilization.

Modern thinking would argue that civilization is opposed to enchantment and, therefore, those who are educated cannot be enchanted. In her essay "Rethinking Mythology," Marcel Detienne observes that today mythology is associated with "the primitive, the inferior races, the peoples of nature, [...] childhood, savagery, madness" (49). In Middle-earth, this is not so. While the Fellowship is in Lothlórien, Celeborn instructs Boromir to not so quickly dismiss old wives' tales, for often such stories contain a memory of things now forgotten by most (*LotR* II.8.374). Characters such as Aragorn, Gandalf, and Elrond understand the influence of Aragorn's legendary blade, Andúril, reforged from the shards of Narsil.[104] It is not the uneducated

---

[104] As you may remember, Narsil was the sword Isildur used to cut the ring from Sauron's finger when he was first defeated.

or superstitious who believe that there are powers at work that cannot be explained, but rather the figures of wisdom, power, and authority.

Moreover, Aragorn's arrival as the rightful king of Gondor demonstrates that the restoration of civilization goes hand in hand with re-enchantment. Long before Aragorn takes the throne, he announces his lineage to Éomer of Rohan. As he draws Andúril and recounts his heritage, he seems to be transformed for a moment into the likeness of one of the great kings of old. Éomer, in shock and awe, mutters, "Dreams and legends spring to life out of the grass" (*LotR* III.2.434).[105] And Éomer is correct — Aragorn's return as king brings to the forefront many powers that had been forgotten. Aragorn reclaims the authority of the *palantíri*, as is his right as king, from the power of Sauron who had used them to corrupt Denethor and Saruman (*LotR* IV.2.780). This signifies the return of the magical and the mystical to the kingdom of Gondor.[106]

Not only does Aragorn return with items of power that are mythic in history and strength, he also has the knowledge to call out the hidden power within familiar things. Faramir, Éowyn, and Merry all suffer from the Black Breath, an ailment inflicted by the Nazgûl, after the battle for Gondor. Aragorn uses kingsfoil, a common weed that the infirmary does not even keep in stock, to call them back. This simple plant is mostly used for headaches, but in the hands of the king it is transformed to combat the darkness of Mordor. Memory of a prophecy that the king will come with miraculous healing is preserved in Gondor only through the tales of an elderly woman (*LotR* V.8.865). Wielding the power of enchantment, Aragorn returns to Gondor. This challenges the conventional assumption that civilization destroys enchantment.

Fantasy as Re-enchantment
In the face of a disenchanted world, Tolkien argues that Fairy-Story, or fantasy, is one primary method to re-enchant our understanding of the world. In "On Fairy-stories," Tolkien explains that "the primal desire at the heart of Faerie [is] the realisation, independent of the conceiving mind, of imagined wonder" (FS 14). Tolkien claims that fantasy enables

---

[105] Our modern world often has disdain and ridicule for legends and the societies that still tell them. Luling recounts her experiences in a small town in Somalia: "There were those who did not want me to write down legends [...] for fear I would publish them and so make their community look ridiculous" (55).

[106] For a fuller exploration of the character of Aragorn and his role in Middle-earth, see Ch. 4, especially the section "Restoration of the True King."

readers to recapture their lost capacity for wonder, providing one avenue to re-enchantment.[107] In sharp contrast to the scientific approach of understanding by dissection, Tolkien lauds fantasy for being "indescribable, though not imperceptible. It has many ingredients, but analysis will not necessarily discover the secret of the whole" (FS 10).[108] For this reason, fantasy is a fundamentally enchanted art form. Although there are discernible pieces (such as plot, narrative, and characters), these features alone do not capture the magic of storytelling.[109]

As disenchantment besets the modern world, those who, like Sam, wish to experience meaning and wonder must seek it elsewhere. In his essay "On Science Fiction," C. S. Lewis explains that those who are "in search of such beauty, awe or terror as the actual world does not supply have been increasingly driven to other planets or other stars" (67–68). Tolkien circumvents the need to depart from our world and enter into a new one to find such experiences through Middle-earth. In one of his letters, Tolkien writes, "Mine is not an 'imaginary' world, but an imaginary historical moment on 'Middle-earth' — which is our habitation" (*Letters* 244). This understanding of Middle-earth creates space to interact with a wonder-filled world not so far removed from our own. We can both enjoy the fantastic elements of Middle-earth and gain real insight about how to interact with our own lives.

Escape through Fantasy

Convinced that Tolkien has created a world that is enchanted and full of vitality, a staunchly disenchanted reader might still insist that Tolkien's work, and all fantasy like it, merely provides a temporary escape from the real world. This accusation that fantasy offers no actual relief is often termed "escapism." In response, Tolkien transforms the connotation of escape. He claims that what fantasy actually provides is "the Escape of the Prisoner," explaining that a prisoner held captive unjustly ought to escape if they can (FS 20). He asserts that escapism accuses readers of "the Flight of the Deserter," implying that readers are running from their responsibilities (FS 20). Fantasy does not deny the harshness of

---

[107] Zeimis expands upon and refines this idea through Tolkien's concept of recovery in the following chapter.

[108] The poem "The Tables Turned" by William Wordsworth also criticizes the scientific approach of understanding by dissection: "Our meddling intellect / Mis-shapes the beauteous forms of things: — / We murder to dissect"(61).

[109] Ch. 1 does a more complete job of addressing Tolkien's narrative techniques.

the disenchanted world; instead, it offers a real possibility of breathing life back into it. Lowentrout concludes that "the most gallant attack mounted by science fiction and fantasy is that which they have made on the meaninglessness that for so long threatened to ring us in" (49). This escape is so much more than a mechanism for distraction or denial. Fantasy has the special ability to reveal truth, particularly fantasy as well-crafted as Tolkien's. *The Lord of the Rings* invites the enchanted and disenchanted alike into the real world of wonder and awe.

In his book, *Orthodoxy*, G. K. Chesterton reflects that it is impossible to reason people out of their coherent views of the world. He uses the example of a person convinced that they are the target of a conspiracy. Any attempt to deny involvement in the conspiracy will simply be met with an irrefutable response: that is exactly what a conspirator would say (Chesterton 24). Any contradictory piece of evidence can fit into this narrative. The only way to reach this person is by convincing them that "although [they are] able to explain a large number of things, [they are] not able to explain them in a large way" (Chesterton 24). This is exactly the predicament in which disenchanted people find themselves. They have consistent but small answers for questions about their place in the world. Although the simple explanation that eventually there will be a scientific answer to every marvelous or miraculous event is impossible to disprove, it confines reality to what the human mind can comprehend.

Further, the person convinced that the entire world is involved in a conspiracy against them is mistaken. The choice between enchantment and disenchantment is not between two neutral and equally accurate interpretations of the world. There is a reality to be perceived and interacted with outside of oneself, and some people see it more accurately than others. Accordingly, Tolkien leaves us with a warning and a hope: Saruman and Ar-Pharazôn incorrectly assess the structure of the world and pay the price, while Gandalf, Aragorn, and others who understand and cooperate with the nature of the world are rewarded. Although it is unlikely that we actually awaken a Balrog or have our homes dismantled by walking trees, there is a grave danger in insisting on a disenchanted worldview. Tolkien enables us to see our world as enchanted, full of the wonder and beauty that is on display in Middle-earth.

Chapter 9

The Road to Recovery
Wyatt Zeimis

THROUGHOUT THE QUEST OF THE RING, Frodo, Sam, Merry, and Pippin experience the novelty and depth of Middle-earth again and again. Each hobbit has multiple encounters with strange beings and foreign races throughout their travels in distant lands. However, they need not travel far from home before encountering strangeness. Shire-life offers little contact with the outside world, and as soon as the hobbits wave goodbye to the valley they call home, their exposure to greater Middle-earth quickly grows.

While still in the Shire, the sound of approaching hooves seems hardly a cause for worry. Nevertheless, Frodo feels an unknown dread, and the hobbits hide among the roots of a tree, hoping the traveler is Gandalf. What they do not know is that one of the Nazgûl made its way into the Shire. As Frodo contends with the pull of the Ring — strengthened by its proximity to the Nazgûl — a false sense of safety tempts him to "slip it on" for he is still surrounded by the familiarity of his home (*LotR* I.3.75).

As they travel through the Shire into Bree and beyond, the hobbits come to realize that familiarity with their surroundings does not protect them from strange encounters. In the Shire, they chance upon elves in the woods who provide safety and company for a night (*LotR* I.3.80). In the Old Forest, the hobbits are offered rest and peace of mind in the house of Tom Bombadil and his wife Goldberry, the ancient and merry master of the forest and daughter of the River (*LotR* I.6.120). They face other dangerous beings close to home, including Old Man Willow and a Barrow-wight (*LotR* I.6.117; I.8.140). Tom Shippey notes that during the hobbits' first real encounters with strange beings, they "are still moving in a very familiar landscape" (*Author* 64). Simply traveling through the region they call home offers a rapid expansion of worldview.

As the hobbits' journey both begins and ends in the Shire, they leave and return thinking it familiar. However, over the course of their journey, the hobbits experience one of Tolkien's most important theories: recovery. Recovery offers the hobbits a deeper understanding of Middle-earth, while also illuminating the underlying truth of our own world through the lens of a fairy story. Although it may not be obvious at first, *The Lord of the Rings* guides both the hobbits and the reader on a road to recovery.

Fantasy, Recovery, Strangeness

Before digging into the nuanced concept of recovery, it is helpful to look at Tolkien's understanding of fantasy.[110] Tolkienian fantasy is a product of sub-creation united with unfamiliarity. It is founded "on a recognition of fact, but not a slavery to it" (FS 55). That is to say, successful fantasy creates a secondary world containing natural things "recognizable from our real-world experience" alongside imagined things not present at all in our primary world (Keys 5).

The act of sub-creation borrows from our reality, reimagining and combining things we are familiar with.[111] These new creations must reflect the nature of their original components because, as Flieger puts it, "we can neither understand nor appreciate a thing we cannot recognize. However apparently alien, however jarring to the imagination, fantasy, to be successful, must be recognizable by the perceiving human consciousness" ("Fantasy and Reality" 5). True fantasy, then, is not a far-flung exploration of the absurd but a creative and intimate perspective on reality.[112]

Fantasy literature is a means of recovery: a way to behold reality in a new light. Recovery results in a deeper understanding of the true nature of things. As Tolkien defines it:

---

[110] As Verlyn Flieger points out in her article "Fantasy and Reality," there is no one definition of fantasy, only an understanding of how each author employs their own theory of fantasy (5).

[111] It is often the case that the fantastic is a means of drawing attention to the novelty in commonplace things. Although fantasy contains both, "Tolkien would rather emphasize the wonder that can be found in commonplace objects than found in creatures of his imagination" (Barkley 17). See Ch. 2 for a deeper analysis of the value in the ordinary.

[112] Tolkien would argue that clear truth and reason uplift fantasy and make it better. The joy of fantasy is found in the truth and connections that can be made between the primary and secondary world (FS 55).

> Recovery [...] is a re-gaining — regaining of a clear view, [...] 'seeing things as we are (or were) meant to see them' — as things apart from ourselves. We need, in any case, to clean our windows; so that the things seen clearly may be freed from the drab blur of triteness or familiarity — from possessiveness (FS 57–58).

Recovery offers a clear view of the primary world, encouraging us to relinquish our assumptions and wonder at the novelty found when the familiar is set free from our expectations (Paroisse). Recovery encourages us to humbly acknowledge that there is often more to understand in things we consider familiar.

Recovery also restores due regard, value, and virtue to that which is recovered (Keys 214). Focusing on things only insofar as they relate to ourselves risks injustice by not acknowledging them in their own right (Keys 214). We must free the familiar from our possession and respect its freedom as something apart from ourselves that can impart truth and wonder (FS 58). Recovery restores ourselves and the familiar to their proper places: closer to truth, open to novelty, and in a constant state of wonder.

We can participate in the sense of recovery in many ways. This could be as simple as giving an extra moment of consideration, as Treebeard does upon hearing Merry and Pippin's voice, instead of assuming they are orcs. Or, it could be as difficult as uprooting societal and cultural stereotypes, such as the Rohirrim encountering the Drúedain. We recover by challenging our assumptions and holding the familiar as if it was new, freeing it to reveal its true nature and elicit fresh wonder (Barkley 17).

The joy of recovery is made possible by arresting strangeness. Arresting strangeness is the way in which the fantastic encourages us to stop and ask, "What is going on here?" (Paroisse). Being "arrested" by a situation, or having to pause due to the strangeness of something, gives us the space to reconcile reality and the fantastic so that we may encounter the joy in fantasy — "a sudden glimpse of the underlying reality or truth" (FS 71). Then, as we assimilate the strange into our understanding, we might practice recovery and see reality anew.

There *is* more than meets the eye — more than we allow ourselves to see in the familiar — which is often "hidden behind our daily business and boredom" (Keys 16). There is strangeness and many unknowns we face, which may change and deepen our understanding of the familiar through recovery. There is also joy and satisfaction found in the pursuit of truth. And there is value in the change caused by recognizing truth — in a deeper understanding of reality and a growing capacity for wonder.[113]

Arresting Strangeness
From Bree onward, the four hobbits are largely surrounded by Men. The Fellowship sets off with Aragorn and Boromir. Sam and Frodo are aided by Faramir and company. Merry becomes an esquire of Rohan, and Pippin becomes a soldier of Gondor. The hobbits grow in familiarity and comfort around Men through these relationships. Two of the hobbits' experiences with Men stand out from the rest and offer a chance for the characters to practice recovery.

The first of these experiences concerns Sam, who, throughout the Quest, has gained familiarity with the potential of Men for both good and evil. Although Sam is quick to distrust Aragorn upon their first meeting in Bree, their friendship grows as Aragorn guides and protects the Fellowship. However, Sam is also witness to the wretchedness of Men through Bill Ferny's mischief-making and Boromir's folly in attempting to take the Ring (*LotR* I.10.165; II.10.399).

Although many of these encounters only hint at Sam's growth, it is plainly seen in his interaction with an enemy. After Sam and Frodo are found by Faramir and company in Ithilien, they are left with two guards away from the fierce ambush laid for the Southrons nearby (*LotR* IV.4.659). As the sound of fighting grows louder, Sam moves closer to see. Suddenly, the dead body of an enemy falls a few feet from him. In this brief moment, Sam is given the opportunity to empathize with the Southron (Luling 56).[114]

Sam's response is to humanize rather than fear him, wondering what his name was, what lies brought him to the warfront, and if he would rather have been home at peace (McFadden 159). Racial and allegiant differences do not diminish this man's humanity. Sam's reaction is also indicative of the goal of the Quest as "the liberation from an evil tyranny of all the 'humane'" (*Letters* 241). This reveals Sam's growth throughout his journey away from home. Sam is no

---

[113] See Ch. 8 for a deeper look into Middle-earth and how it inspires wonder through enchantment.

[114] Notably, this is the only instance in the story where a man under Sauron's dominion is given individuality. Otherwise, the Southrons and Haradrim remain vague, fitting into a stereotype of savage men.

longer the "inexperienced, intolerant, and relatively simple hobbit" who left the Shire months before (Langford 7).

In its brief hold, this moment of empathy highlights humanity's intrinsic worth. Sam momentarily disregards the Southron's association with Sauron and instead practices recovery by seeing him in light of his humanity. Sam sees through the violence and considers the Southron's better nature, recognizing a truth mirrored throughout Middle-earth and the primary world. By dismissing assumptions and recovering his view of Men and the effect of war, Sam demonstrates the virtue found in recovery.

The second experience presents both Merry and the reader with a new group of Men, wholly unlike those met thus far.[115] Upon hearing drums and low voices, Merry anxiously wonders if the enemy is coming. To his surprise, Merry discovers that he is hearing the Drúedain, also known as the Wild Men of the Woods or the Woses — a secluded and ancient group of Men living in the Drúadan Forest.[116] Although considered "remnants of an older time," the Drúedain reflect novel wisdom in their dealings with the Rohirrim (*LotR* V.5.831).

The Drúedain — led by Ghân-buri-Ghân — do not ally with Gondor or Rohan in open war, but lead the Rohirrim on ancient, forgotten paths that circumvent the roads guarded by Sauron's forces. In return, Ghân-buri-Ghân desires that the enemy be defeated and that the Wild Men be left alone (*LotR* V.5.832). As their time together ends, Ghân-buri-Ghân imparts more news about the enemy, notes the changing wind, and departs as suddenly as he came.[117]

Through this passage, it is made clear that there is value in lore and legend. At first, Théoden and Éomer naïvely dismiss Ghân-buri-Ghân's news, thinking they need aid in battle and strength through

---

[115] It is worth noting that all interactions between the Rohirrim and the Drúedain are seen from Merry's unbiased, third-party perspective. We do not gain any greater insight into the personal thoughts or feelings of Théoden and Éomer nor Ghân-buri-Ghân, leaving the reader to discern any underlying tension in their dealings.

[116] The Drúedain resemble Men — although shorter, wider, and rather stumpy — but appear "strange and unlovely" to the Rohirrim. They are skilled and dangerous — knowledgeable about woodcraft and poison — and they hunt Orcs who cross into their forest (*LotR* V.5.832). Tolkien gives a more thorough description of Woses and their history, available in the *Unfinished Tales of Númenor and Middle-earth* (*UT* 277–82).

[117] Notably, no Drúedain was ever seen by any Rider of Rohan again after this interaction (*LotR* V.5.83).

arms. Instead, Ghân-buri-Ghân offers greater help through knowledge of ancient paths. The Drúedain provide aid that is just as valuable as the service of the men on the frontlines. Amid the strangeness surrounding this meeting, Ghân-buri-Ghân restores a regard for lore and legend. That which is considered primitive and unsophisticated may still impart essential truth.

The Drúedain also subvert the Rohirrim's negative perception of them by displaying qualities of wisdom and kindness that disrupt their reputation as "Wild Men" (Kocher 25). Ghân-buri-Ghân extends help in a time of dire need, despite persecution. Their help causes Théoden and the Rohirrim to restore due respect for these ancient people.

Both of these arresting moments reflect the fast-paced nature of life. It is all too easy to gloss over these brief sections in lieu of the larger narrative. Sam does not dwell in the moment with the Southron nor think back to it. The Drúedain are not seen again once they depart.[118] But these examples illustrate the need to discern deeper truths found in even the smallest encounters. Arresting strangeness offers us a chance to reconcile fantasy with reality and let the familiar and the novel impart wisdom.

Reflecting on Trees
The study of nature is another important way to connect a secondary world to the primary. Tolkien was fond of nature and especially of trees. In his letters, he mentions his love for plants, saying that he is always on the side of trees and that the human maltreatment of trees is difficult to bear (*Letters* 220). Tolkien also lovingly describes the significance and transformation of some of the forests in Middle-earth (*Letters* 419–20). The past and present history of Middle-earth is fundamentally entwined with the relationships between beings and trees, which can lead us to restore our view of nature.[119]

Classically, trees hold deep significance throughout fantasy literature. Forests often transcend the natural world and appear as

---

[118] The Drúedain are mentioned again though. As Aragorn and company pass by the Drúadan Forest, they hear beating drums. Then, heralds declare Ghân-buri-Ghân and his folk as the owners of the forest (*LotR* VI.6.976).

[119] The first and most impactful relationship involving trees in the history of Middle-earth is between the Valar and the two trees of Valinor: Telperion and Laurelin. Notably, it is said that "about their fate all the tales of the Elder Days are woven" (*S* 38).

"animated characters" having a life force, vitality, and will of their own (Łaszkiewicz 39).[120] These features encourage suspension of disbelief while offering a restorative view of the significance of the natural world (Łaszkiewicz 55; Flieger, "How Trees Behave" 26–27). Beyond this vital aspect of nature, forests offer encounters with the fantastic that challenge and transform those who travel within (Łaszkiewicz 41, 54). And it can also be the other way around: conscious forests may change and grow through their encounters with travelers. Forests impact many characters throughout the Quest of the Ring, while reflecting a liveliness in the natural world that is often overlooked.

One of the first challenges the four hobbits overcome is their encounter with Old Man Willow in the Old Forest, just outside the Shire. The hobbits are mindful of the Old Forest's strangeness. Merry notes that it is more alive and hateful toward strangers than anything found in the Shire (*LotR* I.6.110). With home behind and the unknown world ahead, the hobbits plod on, allowing the Forest to envelop them in mystery and wonder.

The hobbits eventually arrive at the River Withywindle and are led to Old Man Willow. Slowly, they become overwhelmed by sleepiness under his shade, as if the tree was "singing about sleep" and casting a spell on them (*LotR* I.6.116–17). Soon, Sam finds Frodo in the river, apparently pushed in by the tree, and Merry and Pippin trapped inside the tree trunk. As Sam attempts to free them with fire, Merry exclaims, "Put it out! [...] He'll squeeze me in two if you don't. He says so!" (*LotR* I.6.118). Uttering a desperate cry for help, Frodo and Sam are startled by the sudden arrival of Tom Bombadil. Tom speaks a powerful command over the Old Forest, frees Merry and Pippin, and silences Old Man Willow.

Later, Tom tells the hobbits stories about the Old Forest and Old Man Willow (*LotR* I.7.129). They learn a great deal and behold the trees in a new light. For one, they begin to understand the vast history of the Old Forest as something apart from themselves, realizing that they are strangers in the home of the trees. More than this, Flieger believes Old Man Willow "[makes] actual what the hobbits think they perceive in the trees" ("How Trees Behave" 25). The Old Forest has a consciousness and will full of malice toward those that walk free

---

[120] See Ch. 1 for a closer look at the vitality of land and place within *The Lord of the Rings*.

(*LotR* I.7.130). This experience deepens their understanding of nature as a being outside of themselves.

This is an example of the secondary world maintaining the inner consistency of reality, which leads to recovery. The fantastic Old Forest, in all its strange power, is fundamentally still a forest made up of familiar trees. Yet, it inspires wonderment. It points back to the primary world and encourages us to question how we treat nature and how *it* might feel about us. As the hobbits overcome obstacles and regain a clear view of nature, we are challenged to reflect on our relationship with the natural world.

There is no better way to recover nature than to engage in actual relationships with the natural world, and the Ents provide a means to achieve this. Just before leaving Lórien, Celeborn warns against becoming entangled in the strange land of Fangorn Forest (*LotR* II.8.373–74). Responding to Boromir's confidence in navigating the dangerous forest, Celeborn suggests heeding ancient lore and old wives' tales, for they often preserve truths that were once "needful for the wise to know" (*LotR* II.11.374). This lays subtle groundwork for many characters to wonder at the emergence of the Ents later on. Aragorn is surprised to hear that there is truth in the old tales about tree shepherds — that Ents live on (*LotR* III.5.499). Gandalf chides Théoden for not recognizing the strange Ents, claiming any child could have picked them out of the fireside tales that are told (*LotR* III.8.549). This shows that even simple tales hold deep truth and spark recovery — giving us a chance to suspend disbelief and see the world anew through the lens of a story (Hammond and Scull 335).

Treebeard subverts the negative expectations of Fangorn Forest established by Celeborn and the Old Forest (Łaszkiewicz 46).[121] Treebeard serves as a guardian figure rather than a malicious force hostile to outsiders, such as Old Man Willow.[122] This subversion occurs largely through other characters' ability to engage in a relationship with Treebeard, who is a "vehicle through which Elves, Men, wizards, and hobbits could speak directly to nature" (Stephen L. Walker 4).

---

[121] Another classical component of forests is guardians or a sentient awareness expressing hatred toward mankind, as seen in Old Man Willow.

[122] There is no doubt that Treebeard is still dangerous, for he would have killed Merry and Pippin — taking them for Orcs — had he not first heard their nice voices (*LotR* III.4.464).

Although many characters consider him nothing more than a creature straight out of legend, Treebeard is a link to the natural world.

Whereas Old Man Willow is more realistic — more tree-like — Treebeard requires a greater suspension of disbelief. Flieger believes that, paradoxically, Treebeard is the more believable creature ("How Trees Behave" 26–27). He has depth, personality, and a strong sense of individual identity. Treebeard is relatable. We recognize Treebeard because we recognize both trees and humans — we can comprehend the sub-creation of a rational being with treelike features. Further, we are invited to understand Fangorn's plight and grow in concern for the trees. The reader is encouraged to let familiar nature become strange.

Merry and Pippin are initially afraid upon meeting Treebeard, but they are soon set at ease — particularly by his deep, attentive, and caring eyes — and their fear is replaced with curiosity (*LotR* III.4.464). The experience of these hobbits thus far has developed a "deeper and perhaps even habitual capacity for awe at the strange" (Keys 213). It is important that Pippin feels a "curious suspense" during this meeting because it reveals his desire to see more in the familiar (*LotR* III.4.464). "Curious" because he is open to and interested in learning more about Treebeard. "Suspense" because there is anticipation and excitement in knowing the truth, especially regarding an ancient, novel mixture of tree and man. Merry and Pippin practice recovery as they reconcile his familiarity and his strangeness.

It may be easy to assume that someone as ancient and wise as Treebeard would have little reason to practice recovery. He has lived through many ages and has come to know Middle-earth intimately. But in fact, the Ents live a life of constant recovery, which is hinted at in Treebeard's acceptance of the hobbits. When he cannot place the hobbits in an old list of beings he learned when he was young, he acknowledges that they may have been included in a new list made since then (*LotR* III.4.464). He recognizes the hobbits and accepts their identity as novel beings in Middle-earth. When the hobbits are met by other races — namely Men — they are dismissed as Halflings, or little people found merely in tales (Stephen L. Walker 5).[123] Treebeard, on the other hand, has a different approach, which is a representation of "the world's awakening to and by [the hobbits]" (Stephen L. Walker 5).

---

[123] See also *LotR* III.2.434, III.8.557, and V.1.755.

There is more to Hobbits than meets the eye.[124] There is also more to Treebeard — and nature as an extension — than there seems to be.

Treebeard displays a unique proclivity for recovery in yet another way: through the Ents' understanding of names. Whereas the hobbits share their names freely, Treebeard is more guarded in offering his real name. In Old Entish "real names tell you the story of the things they belong to," and they are always growing throughout life (*LotR* III.4.465). Ents can never be fully known — there is always more being added to their life experience and thus to their name. The Ents' use of names requires them to continuously recover their fellow Ents.

More than just challenging characters to grow and recover, forests also direct our attention to humankind's greater relationship with nature. Time and time again nature is exploited for trivial gain (Łaszkiewicz 49). Saruman's violence against Fangorn is a travesty worthy of Treebeard's attention as well as our own.[125] If we are to regain a clear view of the world, we must be willing to confront the evil that occurs within it. Saruman and his forces lay waste to the beautiful forest surrounding Isengard, to trees who had voices of their own (*LotR* III.4.474). Saruman desires to mold nature to his will rather than accept it as is and behold its inherent value. Saruman strays from his role as steward of Middle-earth and selfishly takes from the environment at nature's expense (Goetsch 7). The Ents justifiably rise up and put a stop to Isengard's evil actions.

In the same way, humanity must steward the earth. Tolkien writes, "every tree has its enemy, few have an advocate" (*Letters* 321). In the case of Fangorn, we see the trees as able to advocate for themselves, but it is not so in our world. The destruction of nature for naïve, selfish progress should elicit anger and opposition, much as it does in Treebeard. Deforestation and environmental harm are realities of the world that need to be faced for the sake of nature and ourselves. The value of trees throughout Middle-earth reflects our world's nature and is a cause for recovery.

Recovery Revealed
Recovery elicits fresh wonder for many characters, but its effects are not limited to those in the story. The mere act of reading *The Lord of the Rings*

---

[124] See Ch. 2 for an analysis of how Hobbits are thought to be an ordinary, unassuming race, yet they display unique and valuable qualities.

[125] See Ch. 8 and Harbman's section "A Disenchanted Wizard" for a look into Saruman's mistreatment of the natural world.

can cause the reader to experience recovery themselves again and again. In many cases, we are led to assumptions that are later subverted in ways that reflect the truth and wonder found through recovery. As we witness recovery in action alongside the Fellowship, the narrative enables readers to regain a clear view of Middle-earth and our own world.

One event where the reader may experience recovery occurs early on in the hobbits' journey. On their way out of the Shire, the four hobbits hear approaching hooves. Ill at ease, they hide on the side of the road (*LotR* I.3.74). As it turns out, a Nazgûl comes along and the hobbits narrowly avoid an encounter that might have ended the Quest before it began. This leads us to be wary of strangers going forward.

Finally, the hobbits safely reach Farmer Maggot's land, stay for dinner, and pile in his wagon to be driven to Bucklebury Ferry (*LotR* I.4.95). As they approach the water, they hear hoofbeats once again from out of the fog. Fearing for their lives, they hide in the wagon and listen to the stranger inquire about a Mr. Baggins — just as the Nazgûl had done. This familiar situation sets us up to believe that the new stranger is also a Nazgûl. Thankfully, the voice of the stranger gives him away as none other than Merry Brandybuck. At first, we assume this stranger is an enemy, but if we look again, it is also plausible that he is a friend, since the hobbits are still near home. A potentially dangerous situation turns into a joyous reunion, and we are relieved when the truth is revealed.

Another example where the reader experiences recovery through subverted expectations is seen in Aragorn, Gimli, and Legolas's confrontation with a mysterious man in Fangorn Forest. While sitting around the firelight of their camp, Gimli glimpses an old man, cloaked and leaning on a great staff just out of the light's reach (*LotR* III.2.442). Aragorn cries out for the man to join them, but he disappears without making a sound. This encounter leads them to believe that the man must have been Saruman or "an evil phantom" of him (*LotR* III.5.488). The old man is later confirmed to have been Saruman, but subtle hints lead both the characters and the reader to question whether or not it was truly him until we are told so (*LotR* III.5.498).[126]

---

[126] The hints are that the man had a hat, not a hood, that their horses sounded joyful as they fled, and that he left no trace (*LotR* III.2.443; III.5.488). Gandalf confirms that it was Saruman who they saw earlier and explains that he left Orthanc, eager to meet the captured hobbits, thinking they had the Ring, but had arrived too late after their escape. The old man is also confirmed to be Saruman in

After entering the forest, Legolas sees an old man once again, and, assuming it is Saruman, they prepare to defend themselves. The man approaches, wishing to speak, and he tells them about the hobbits they are pursuing (*LotR* III.5.494). He then draws back his cloak and reveals shining white garments beneath, a sure sign that he is Saruman the White. Suddenly, Legolas cries out "Mithrandir!" for indeed, it is Gandalf! We learn that Gandalf has become all that Saruman should have been (*LotR* III.5.495). Both the characters and the reader are surprised to discover that the old man in the forest is not Saruman, and even more surprised when he is revealed as Gandalf returned. In this wondrous meeting, we experience recovery when what we think is familiar reveals a deeper truth.

The narrative prompts us to recover rather than simply showing us examples of recovery. We are encouraged to release our own expectations and assumptions, while being witness to recovery as the familiar is cast in a new light again and again. *The Lord of the Rings* is full of relatable truth that we can also see in our world — a valuable lesson within a priceless narrative.

Returning Home

At the end of the tale, readers find themselves alongside the hobbits, journeying back home — a return to comfort and familiarity. However, what was once familiar has changed in their absence, and the travelers who set out so long ago have been transformed by the journey. Recognizing this reality as they return home creates an opportunity to practice recovery and appreciate the novelty found in the familiar.

In a meta-narrative about the story they are in, Sam describes a good end to a tale as being a return home, where things there are all right, but not exactly the same (*LotR* IV.8.711). This is a desirable end for those in the story but not always as exciting for those who hear it. Much later on in their journey home, Frodo shares the reality that despite returning home, it will no longer be familiar because he is not the same hobbit who set out from the Shire many months prior (*LotR* VI.7.989). As the hobbits recover their home, they also discover truths about themselves and their place in the world.

Upon returning home, the hobbits find the Shire in disarray under the oppression of Saruman and his ruffians. Things are not

---

one of Tolkien's early time-schemes (Hammond and Scull 374).

familiar nor are they going well. Luckily, the hobbits have been empowered by their journey to prevail over the evils at home. Merry and Pippin, in particular, take up the role as leaders in handling the ruffians.[127] After rousing the Shire and overthrowing their oppressors, the Hobbit community attempts to restore the damage done.

Saruman's subjugation offers Shire-folk a clear view of the reality of danger in Middle-earth — something they had little contact with before since they had lived under the unseen protection of the Rangers. This violent intrusion into Shire life is finally stopped by the hobbits who journey back again, armed with proper preparation and new knowledge of the world around them (Langford 9). Similarly, the restoration of the Shire is led by these same hobbits who offer the Shire-folk a clear view of greater Middle-earth. They bring back with them stories and songs. They also re-establish meaningful leadership; Sam becomes Mayor; Merry, the Master of Buckland; Pippin, Took and Thain. They are appointed Counselors of the North-kingdom under the authority of King Elessar (*LotR* App.B.1097). The *mallorn* tree that grows from Galadriel's gift to Sam is a connection to the unique and vibrant nature outside the Shire that travelers and hobbits from all around marvel at (*LotR* VI.9.1023). The Shire thrives with an enchanting beauty, growth, and richness that seems divine. From the perspective of the returning hobbits though, home becomes a far different place from what they pictured while they were away.

Frodo comes to realize that he no longer has a place in the Shire and that there is a home better suited for him in the West across the sea. He accepts that he saved the Shire — as was his desire from the beginning — but realizes it is no longer his (*LotR* VI.9.1029).[128] Rather, the fulfillment of the Quest gives the Shire back to the Hobbits under the restorative governance of Sam, Merry, and Pippin. Through them, the Shire becomes more than it ever was, though they also leave at some point to places more appropriate for them. Sam follows Frodo into the West as the last Ring-bearer. Merry and Pippin travel and live their final days in Gondor and are laid beside the great of Gondor

---

[127] See Mar's section "Ordinary Battles" in Ch. 2 for an analysis of Merry and Pippin's growth throughout the narrative, leading up to their preparedness to reclaim the Shire.

[128] Frodo chose to set out from the Shire with the Ring in part to save his home and in part to see Bilbo again (*LotR* I.2.62). Read more about their relationship in Bunnel's section "Familial Connections" in Ch. 3.

upon death (*LotR* App.B.1096–98). They all outgrow and eventually relinquish the Shire as their own home, all the while gaining a clear understanding of their identity. As the hobbits practice recovery, they realize they have a different life ahead of them — a new home that offers proper restoration.

When we look at reality expecting familiarity but find strangeness, there is nothing necessarily wrong with it, nor with us. Perhaps we have simply gained a clear view of our world. Recovering the familiar does not guarantee it the same place in our lives. With recovery comes the responsibility to respond with our new understanding of reality. We cannot continue living under our old assumptions; rather, something has to change in our lives so we can reconcile and accept the new truths we find. Often, the growth that comes with recovery leads us toward a more proper place in the world. Recovery is a journey that is never truly over.

As we journey back again to Middle-earth and eventually return to our own world, we may find ourselves looking at reality from a new perspective. Having experienced recovery and the growth it produces, we now have a responsibility to live a life characterized by recovery. We must challenge our assumptions through openness to novelty and a willingness to be changed by it. Middle-earth equips us to seek more in our world — because there will always be more to see and to wonder at anew.

Epilogue
Wyatt Zeimis and Jensen A. Kirkendall

WHEN WE ASKED OURSELVES what should be written about *The Lord of the Rings*, we decided on a seemingly simple idea: it is worth reading more than once. Our primary focus was not cutting-edge research nor unheard-of insights. Each chapter in *Journey Back Again* proposes one angle, one theme, one vein of study to stimulate deeper consideration of Tolkien's masterpiece. We sought to offer an introduction to the rich themes and ideas that Tolkien studies seeks to illuminate, while adding a few new insights and sparking ideas of our own. Our foundational hope is that our reader is left with an eagerness to go back to Tolkien's work.

We, a fellowship of nine ourselves, felt this eagerness in our own writing process, gaining a great deal from Tolkien's world as we worked together. In this process, our work became far more than an academic endeavor — our project became inherently relational. Dr. Diana Pavlac Glyer, our editor, mentor, and loremaster, firmly and consistently emphasized that our reading, writing, and discussion were about the people more than the project, coming together first as friends and then as scholars. Accordingly, we researched together, sometimes laughing over a meal, other times debating in the classroom, but always with a shared goal of collective growth and learning. We discovered that the burdens and blessings of collaboration in Tolkien's Fellowship ring true in our own lives, for they parallel our collaborative experience. Through this process, we created a book of scholarship alongside deep-rooted trust in one another's friendship. We hope this shines through alongside our scholarly endeavors.

Dr. Glyer has devoted decades to demonstrating the way Tolkien influenced and was influenced by his writing group, the Inklings. She collected her deep, careful research into *The Company They Keep* (2007), proving the ways the members of the Inklings influenced each other. She then introduced her ideas to a wider audience in the more application-oriented *Bandersnatch* (2016), attempting to help people develop their own creative communities. Both of these works demonstrate Dr. Glyer's simple but powerful claim that creativity thrives in community. In addition to her personal scholarship, we hope Dr. Glyer can point to *Journey Back Again* as further proof of her argument.

We nine authors, under her guidance, discovered exactly what she argued years earlier — that "the most common and natural expressions of creativity occur as part of an ongoing dialogue between writers, readers, texts, and contexts. [...] Like filaments joined together in a web, writers work as members of large communities. As they work, they influence and are influenced by the company they keep" (*The Company They Keep* 226). Collaboration took us farther than we ever could have imagined going alone. With Dr. Glyer and Tolkien as our guides, we learned for ourselves that creativity thrives in community. We hope our collaboration is yet another series of filaments joining you and others into this conversation.

In accordance with this focus, *Journey Back Again* seeks to be holistic in its scholarship. As scholars, we came with our emotions, our philosophical quandaries, our cultural anxieties, our religious practices, and our social longings to journey through Tolkien's world. Scholars are not satisfied with surfaces but delve deeper, seeking a robust and multi-valenced understanding. We have found that the most rich and engaging scholarship goes just a little bit farther than knowledge, including a suggestion of real-world application. We research, we teach, we study, we learn — but then we can ask, how might we live differently based on these new insights? This central question drove us, bearing in mind all our individual and corporate lines of inquiry, to immerse ourselves in Tolkien's story. In addition to each of the chapter subjects, we found that one of the most powerful aspects of *The Lord of the Rings* is that it moved us — for this is the relentless worth of story in all its forms: its unending potential to move us at the various levels of our humanity.

We hope *Journey Back Again* exemplifies what we believe to be the true heart of scholarship: community, collaboration, and conversation. While the academic world can be a peculiar, thorny place, we feel firmly that scholarship also possesses an unending potential. We ourselves feel acutely that our work leaves many avenues of thought unexplored. As *Journey Back Again* took shape, there were many subjects we had to set aside, such as questions of estrangement and reconciliation, the strange call of the Elves to the West, and the deep life of Middle-earth's natural world. Many other scholars continue to pursue various important lines of inquiry, including John Garth, Dimitra Fimi, Carl F. Hostetter, Thomas Honegger, and Tom Shippey, to name but a few. Our book is a preliminary dialogue within a robust and developing scholarly community. We hope our readers do not stop here but continue their journey with Tolkien alongside us and other scholars.

This epilogue adds one final takeaway from our journey through *The Lord of the Rings*: a journey back to Middle-earth, based on our experience, is best done in community. Read *The Lord of the Rings*; read it again; read it aloud; but above all, read it with friends. None of our heroes in Middle-earth go it alone, and if they tried Master Samwise would surely be there anyway. We have gained what we have gained from Middle-earth because we read it, reveled in it, and wrestled with it together. We now encourage you to allow your community, alongside Tolkien's story, to show you something new each time you set out. Whatever directions future Tolkien scholarship takes, we hope the paths are wide enough for many to walk side by side. A journey is better and the world is larger with friends to walk alongside — the ones you set out with and the ones you meet along the way.

Works Cited

Alberto, Maria. "'It Had Been His Virtue, and Therefore also the Cause of His Fall': Seduction as a Mythopoeic Accounting for Evil in Tolkien's Work." *Mythlore*, vol. 35, no. 2, 15 Apr. 2017, pp. 63–79, dc.swosu.edu/mythlore/vol35/iss2/5.

Aracil, Leticia Cortina. "Shadow Shrouds and Moonlight Veils: The Forest as an Existential Scene in Tolkien's Legendarium." *Beasts of the Forest: Denizens of the Dark Woods*, edited by Jon Hackett and Seán Harrington, Indiana UP, 2019, books.google.com/books/about/Beasts_of_the_Forest.html?id=1Oe9DwAAQBAJ.

Arendt, Hannah. *The Human Condition.* 2nd ed., 1958. Reprint, U of Chicago P, 1998.

Aristotle. *Nicomachean Ethics.* Translated with an introduction and notes by Martin Ostwald, Prentice Hall, 1999.

Arthur, Elizabeth. "Above All Shadows Rides the Sun: Gollum as Hero." *Mythlore*, vol. 18, no. 1, 15 Oct. 1991, pp. 19–27, dc.swosu.edu/mythlore/vol18/iss1/4.

Baker, Dallas John. "Writing Back to Tolkien: Gender, Sexuality, and Race in High Fantasy." *Recovering History through Fact and Fiction: Forgotten Lives*, edited by Dallas John Baker, Donna Lee Brien, and Nike Sulway, Cambridge Scholars Publishing, 2017, pp. 123–144, www.google.com/books/edition/Recovering_History_through_Fact_and_Fict/WPlVDwAAQBAJ?hl=en&gbpv=1.

Barkan, Steven E. "1.3 Theoretical Perspectives in Sociology." *Sociology: Brief Edition*, 2012, 2012books.lardbucket.org/books/sociology-brief-edition-v1.1/s04-03-theoretical-perspectives-in-so.html.

Barkley, Christine. "Predictability and Wonder: Familiarity and Recovery in Tolkien's Works." *Mythlore*, vol. 8, no. 1, 15 Apr. 1981, pp. 16–18, dc.swosu.edu/mythlore/vol8/iss1/2.

Bauman, Zygmunt. *Intimations of Postmodernity.* Routledge, 1992.

BBC News. "How Facebook updated its 'six degrees of separation' (it's now 3.57)." 5 Feb. 2016, www.bbc.com/news/newsbeat-35500398.

Berry, Wendell. *Bringing It to the Table: On Farming and Food*. Counterpoint Press, 2009.

Bramlett, Perry C. *I Am in Fact a Hobbit: An Introduction to the Life and Works of J. R. R. Tolkien*. Mercer UP, 2003.

Branchaw, Sherrylyn. "Boromir: Breaker of the Fellowship?" *Tolkien Studies*, vol. 12, no. 1, 2015, pp. 123–40, doi.org/10.1353/tks.2015.0006.

Bratman, David. Review of *Sub-creating Arda: World-building in J. R. R. Tolkien's Work, Its Precursors, and Its Legacies*, edited by Dimitra Fimi and Thomas Honegger. *Tolkien Studies*, vol. 16, 2019, pp 174–78, *Project MUSE*, doi.org/10.1353/tks.2019.0014.

Brooke-Rose, Christine. "The Evil Ring: Realism and the Marvelous." *Poetics Today*, vol 1, no. 4, 1980, pp. 67–90, www.jstor.org/stable/1771887.

Brown, Devin. "From Isolation to Community: Frodo's Incomplete Personal Quest in *The Lord of the Rings*." *Mythlore*, vol. 25, no. 1, 15 Oct. 2006, pp. 163–74, dc.swosu.edu/mythlore/vol25/iss1/12.

Caldecott, Stratford. "The Horns of Hope: J. R. R. Tolkien and the Heroism of Hobbits." *The Chesterton Review*, vol. 28, no. 1, 2002, pp. 29–55, doi.org/10.5840/chesterton2002281/29.

———. *The Power of the Ring: The Spiritual Vision Behind* The Lord of the Rings *and* The Hobbit. 2nd ed., Crossroad Publishing, 2012.

Carpenter, Humphrey. *J. R. R. Tolkien: A Biography*. Houghton Mifflin Harcourt Publishing, 2000.

Catanach, Dawn. "The Problem of Éowyn: A Look at Ethics and Values in Middle-earth." *The Grey Book*, vol. 1, 2005, pp. 1–5, www.academia.edu/12328053/The_Problem_of_Éowyn_A_L_ook_at_Ethics_and_Values_in_Middle-earth.

Chance, Jane. "*The Lord of the Rings*: Tolkien's Epic." *Tolkien's Art: A Mythology for England*, UP of Kentucky, 2001, pp. 141–83, www.jstor.org/stable/j.ctt2jch8t.

———. "Power and the Community: *The Return of the King*." Lord of the Rings: *The Mythology of Power*, UP of Kentucky, 2001, pp. 95–127, www.jstor.org/stable/j.ctt2jct9b.9.

Chesterton, G. K. *Orthodoxy*. Ignatius Press, 1995.

Cicero, Marcus Tullius. *Cicero De Amicitia (On Friendship) and Scipio's Dream*. Translated with an introduction and notes by Andrew P. Peabody, Little and Brown, 1887. oll.libertyfund.org/titles/544.

———. *On the Good Life*. Translated with an introduction by Michael Grant, Penguin Books, 1971.

Confucius. *The Analects of Confucius*. Translated and annotated by Arthur Waley, Random House, 1989.

Cosper, Mike. *Recapturing the Wonder: Transcendent Faith in a Disenchanted World*. InterVarsity Press, 2017.

Coutras, Lisa. *Tolkien's Theology of Beauty: Majesty, Splendor, and Transcendence in Middle-earth*. Palgrave Macmillan, 2016.

Croft, Janet Brennan. "The Name of the Ring: or, There and Back Again." *Mythlore*, vol. 35, no. 2, 15 Apr. 2017, pp. 81–94, dc.swosu.edu/mythlore/vol35/iss2/6.

Davison, Scott A. "Tolkien and the Nature of Evil." *The Lord of the Rings and Philosophy: One Ring to Rule Them All*, edited by Gregory Bassham and Eric Bronson, Open Court Publishing, 2003, pp. 99–109.

"Despair, v.," *OED Online*, Oxford UP, Mar. 2022, oed.com/view/Entry/50936.

Detienne, Marcel. "Rethinking Mythology." *Between Belief and Transgression: Structuralist Essays in Religion, History, and Myth*, edited by M. Izard and P. Smith, U of Chicago P, 1982.

Deyo, Steven Mark. "Wyrd and Will: Fate, Fatalism, and Free Will in The Northern Elegy and J. R. R. Tolkien." *Mythlore*, vol. 14, no. 3, 15 Mar. 1988, pp. 59–62, dc.swosu.edu/mythlore/vol14/iss3/11.

Dickerson, Matthew T. *Following Gandalf: Epic Battles and Moral Victory in* The Lord of the Rings. Brazos Press, 2003.

Dickerson, Matthew T., and Jonathan Evans. *Ents, Elves, and Eriador: The Environmental Vision of J. R. R. Tolkien*. UP of Kentucky, 2006.

Donnelly, Colleen. "Feudal Values, Vassalage, and Fealty in *The Lord of the Rings*." *Mythlore*, vol. 25, no. 3, 15 Apr. 2007, pp. 17–27, dc.swosu.edu/mythlore/vol25/iss3/3.

Drury, Rogery. "Providence at Elrond's Council." *Mythlore*, vol. 7, no. 3, 15 Oct. 1980, pp. 8–9. dc.swosu.edu/mythlore/vol7/iss3/4.

Dubs, Kathleen E. "Providence, Fate, and Chance: Boethian Philosophy in *The Lord of the Rings*." *Twentieth Century Literature*, vol. 27, no. 1, 1981, pp. 34–42, doi.org/10.2307/441084.

Ducey, Mary K. "Principles of Ultimate Reality and Meaning in the Legendarium of J. R. R. Tolkien: Pity and Mercy." *Ultimate Reality and Meaning*, vol. 34, nos. 3–4, Jan. 2011, pp. 286–303, doi.org/10.3138/uram.34.3-4.286.

Evans, G. R. *Augustine on Evil*. Cambridge UP, 1982.

"Evil, adj. and n.1." *OED Online*, Oxford UP, Mar. 2022, oed.com/view/Entry/65386.

Fimi, Dimitra. *Tolkien, Race and Cultural History: From Fairies to Hobbits*. Palgrave Macmillan, 2010.

Fimi, Dimitra, and Thomas Honegger, editors. *Sub-creating Arda: World-building in J. R. R. Tolkien's Work, its Precursors and its Legacies*. Walking Tree Publishers, 2019.

Flieger, Verlyn. "Fantasy and Reality: J. R. R. Tolkien's World and the Fairy-Story Essay." *Mythlore*, vol. 22, no. 3, 15 Oct. 1999, pp. 4–13, dc.swosu.edu/mythlore/vol22/iss3/2.

———. "Frodo and Aragorn: The Concept of the Hero." *Understanding The Lord of the Rings: The Best of Tolkien Criticism*, edited by Rose A. Zimbardo and Neil D. Isaacs, Houghton Mifflin, 2004, pp. 122–45.

———. "How Trees Behave — Or Do They?" *Mythlore*, vol. 32, no. 1, 2013, pp. 21–34, dc.swosu.edu/mythlore/vol32/iss1/3.

Frye, Northrop. *Anatomy of Criticism: Four Essays*, 15th ed., with a new foreword by Harold Bloom, Princeton UP, 1957.

Garth, John. *Tolkien and the Great War: The Threshold of Middle-earth*. Houghton Mifflin, 2003.

Genette, Gérard. *Narrative Discourse: An Essay in Method*. Translated by Jane E. Lewin, Cornell UP, 1980.

Glyer, Diana Pavlac. *Bandersnatch: C. S. Lewis, J. R. R. Tolkien, and the Creative Collaboration of the Inklings*. Kent State UP, 2016.

———. *The Company They Keep: C. S. Lewis and J. R. R. Tolkien as Writers in Community*. Kent State UP, 2007.

Goetsch, Richard. "Environmental Stewardship in the Works of J. R. R. Tolkien." Trinity Evangelical Divinity School, 2012, www.academia.edu/1825597/Environmental_Stewardship_in_the_Works_of_J.R.R._Tolkien.

Greenwood, Linda. "Love: 'The Gift of Death.'" *Tolkien Studies*, vol. 2, 2005, pp. 171–95, doi.org/10.1353/tks.2005.0019.

Guerrero, Laura K., et al. *Close Encounters: Communication in Relationships*. 4th ed., SAGE Publications, 2014.

Hall, Mark R. "Gandalf and Merlin, Aragorn and Arthur: Tolkien's Transmogrification of the Arthurian Tradition and Its Use as a Palimpsest for *The Lord of the Rings*." *Inklings Forever*, vol. 8, no. 1, 2012, pp. 1–10, pillars.taylor.edu/inklings_forever/vol8/iss1/6.

Hamilton, Gillian, et al. "Building Community for the Long Term: An Intergenerational Commitment." *The Gerontologist,* vol. 39, no. 2, Apr. 1999, pp. 235–38, doi.org/10.1093/geront/39.2.235.

Hammond, Wayne G., and Christina Scull. The Lord of the Rings: *A Reader's Companion.* Houghton Mifflin Harcourt, 2005.

Hatzfeld, Katherine. "The Legolas/Gimli Binary: The Role of Memory and Nature for Racial Reconciliation in *Lord of the Rings.*" Presented at Mythcon 50 at San Diego State U in San Diego, CA, 2 Aug. 2019.

Hick, John. *Evil and the God of Love.* Harper & Row, 1966.

Hills, Peter, and Michael Argyle. "Happiness, Introversion-Extraversion and Happy Introverts." *Personality and Individual Differences,* vol. 30, no. 4, Mar. 2001, pp. 595–608, doi.org/10.1016/S0191-8869(00)00058-1.

Hirsch, Bernhard. "After the 'end of all things': The Long Return Home to the Shire." *Tolkien Studies,* vol. 11, 2014, pp. 77–107, doi.org/10.1353/tks.2014.0015.

Hofweber, Thomas. "Logic and Ontology." *The Stanford Encyclopedia of Philosophy,* edited by Edward N. Zalta, 2017, plato.stanford.edu/entries/logic-ontology.

Honegger, Thomas. "Splintered Heroes — Heroic Variety and its Function in *The Lord of the Rings.*" *A Wilderness of Dragons: Essays in Honor of Verlyn Flieger,* edited by John D. Rateliff, Gabbro Head Press, 2018.

———. "'Uncle me no uncle!' Or Why Bilbo Is and Isn't Frodo's Uncle." *Journal of Tolkien Research,* vol. 9, no. 1, 2020, pp. 1–11, scholar.valpo.edu/journaloftolkienresearch/vol9/iss1/4.

Hopkins, Gerard Manley. "God's Grandeur." *Hopkins: Poems and Prose,* vol. 14, Penguin Random House, 1995.

Houghton, John Wm, and Neal K. Keesee. "Tolkien, King Alfred, and Boethius: Platonist Views of Evil in *The Lord of The Rings.*" *Tolkien Studies,* vol. 2, 2005, pp. 131–59, doi.org/10.1353/tks.2005.0021.

Johnson, Brent D. "Éowyn's Grief." *Mythlore,* vol. 27, no. 3, 15 Apr. 2009, pp. 117–27, dc.swosu.edu/mythlore/vol27/iss3/15.

Keys, Mary M. "J. R. R. Tolkien's *The Hobbit, Or, There and Back Again*: Recovering a Platonic-Aristotelian Politics of Friendship in Liberal Democracy." *Homer Simpson Ponders Politics: Popular Culture as Political Theory,* edited by Joseph J. Foy and Timothy M. Dale, UP of Kentucky, 2013, pp. 203–32, www.jstor.org/stable/j.ctt2tv5xb.16.

Kilby, Clyde S. *Tolkien and* The Silmarillion. Harold Shaw Publishers, 1976.

Kisor, Yvette. "Incorporeality and Transformation in *The Lord of the Rings.*" *The Body in Tolkien's Legendarium: Essays on Middle-earth Corporeality*, edited by Christopher Vaccaro, McFarland, 2013, pp. 20–39.

Kocher, Paul H. "The Drúedain." *Mythlore*, vol. 10, no. 3, Jan. 1984, pp. 23–25, dc.swosu.edu/mythlore/vol10/iss3/6.

Kreeft, Peter. *The Philosophy of Tolkien: The Worldview Behind* The Lord of the Rings. Ignatius Press, 2005.

Langford, Jonathan D. "The Scouring of the Shire as a Hobbit Coming-of-Age." *Mythlore: A Journal of J. R. R. Tolkien, C. S. Lewis, Charles Williams and Mythopoeic Literature*, vol. 18, no. 1, 15 Oct. 1991, pp. 4–9, dc.swosu.edu/mythlore/vol18/iss1/1.

LaSala, Jeff. "In Defense of Tolkien's Deus Ex Machina." *TOR.com*, 27 Dec. 2017, www.tor.com/2017/12/27/in-defense-of-tolkiens-deus-ex-machina.

Łaszkiewicz, Weronika. "Into the Wild Woods: On the Significance of Trees and Forests in Fantasy Fiction." *Mythlore*, vol. 36, no. 1, Oct. 2017, pp. 39–58, dc.swosu.edu/mythlore/vol36/iss1/4.

Latour, Bruno. *We Have Never Been Modern*. Translated by Catherine Porter, Harvard UP, 1993.

Lewis, C. S. "Edmund Spenser, 1552–99." *Studies in Medieval and Renaissance Literature*, collected by Walter Hooper, Cambridge UP, 1998, pp. 121–45.

———. *The Four Loves*. 1960. Reprint, Harcourt Books, 1988.

———. "On Science Fiction." *Of Other Worlds: Essays and Stories*, Harcourt Brace Jovanovich, 1975, pp. 59–73.

———. "On Stories." *On Stories: And Other Essays on Literature*, edited by Walter Hooper, Houghton Mifflin Harcourt, 1982, pp. 3–20, ebookcentral.proquest.com/lib/apu/detail.action?docID=3302095.

———. *The Voyage of the Dawn Treader*. HarperCollins Publishers, 1952.

Leyerle, John. "The Interlace Structure of *Beowulf.*" *University of Toronto Quarterly*, vol. 37, no. 1, Oct. 1967, pp. 1–17, www.muse.jhu.edu/article/571732.

Lowentrout, Peter. "The Rags of Lordship: Science Fiction, Fantasy, and the Reenchantment of the World." *Mythlore*, vol. 11, no. 3, 15 Feb. 1985, pp. 47–57, dc.swosu.edu/mythlore/vol11/iss3/9.

Luling, Virginia. "An Anthropologist in Middle-earth." *Mythlore*, vol. 21, no. 2, 15 Oct. 1996, pp. 53–57, dc.swosu.edu/mythlore/vol21/iss2/11.

McFadden, Brian. "The Swertings and Racial Difference." *Tolkien's Modern Middle Ages*, edited by Jane Chance and Alfred K. Siewers, Palgrave Macmillan, 2005.

"Mercy, n." *OED Online*, Oxford UP, Mar. 2022, www.oed.com/view/Entry/116713.

Moe, Kristen Fuglesteg. "Speak, Friend, and Enter: Interracial Friendship in the Works of J. R. R. Tolkien." Master's thesis, U of Bergen, 2016, hdl.handle.net/1956/12389.

Moseley, Charles. "A World of Words." *J. R. R. Tolkien*, edited by Charles Moseley, Liverpool UP, 1997, doi.org/10.2307/j.ctv5rf2gb.

Nelson, Charles W. "But Who is Rose Cotton? — Love and Romance in *The Lord of the Rings*." *Journal of the Fantastic in the Arts*, vol 3, nos. 3–4, 1994, pp. 6–20, www.jstor.org/stable/43308193.

New Catholic Encyclopedia. 8th ed., Thomson Gale, 2003.

Northrup, Clyde B. "The Qualities of a Tolkienian Fairy-Story." *Modern Fiction Studies*, vol. 50, no. 4, 2004, pp. 814–37, doi.org/10.1353/mfs.2005.0007.

Nussbaum, Martha C. *Love's Knowledge: Essays on Philosophy and Literature*. Oxford UP, 1990.

Nystrom-Schut, Michael Jean. *Principles of Philosophy: The Balanced Life, Volume 1*. AuthorHouse, 2018. www.google.com/books/edition/Principles_of_Philosophy/Ks1zvQEACAAJ?hl=en.

Paroisse Ste-Anne. "The Immaculate Conception, John the Baptist, and Arresting Strangeness." *Paroisse Ste-Anne*, 8 Dec. 8, 2018, stannemattawa.com/articles/2018/12/8/the-immaculate-conception-john-the-baptist-and-arresting-strangeness.

Partridge, Christopher. *The Re-enchantment of the West Vol. 2: Alternative Spiritualities, Sacralization, Popular Culture, and Occulture*. T and T Clark, 2005.

Petersen-Deeprose, Danna. "'Something Mighty Queer': Destabilizing Cishetero Amatonormativity in the Works of Tolkien." Virtual Presentation at Tolkien Society, Summer Seminar 2021, 4 July 2021.

Powell, David C. "Tolkien's *The Silmarillion*: A Reexamination of Providence." Master's thesis, Florida Atlantic U, 2009, www.worldcat.org/oclc/824560529.

Robinson, Howard. "Dualism." *The Stanford Encyclopedia of Philosophy*, edited by Edward N. Zalta, 2016, plato.stanford.edu/archives/sum2018/entries/dualism.

Ruane, Abigail E., and Patrick James. *The International Relations of Middle-earth: Learning from* The Lord of the Rings. U of Michigan P, 2012. www.fulcrum.org/concern/monographs/z890rv062.

Rutledge, Fleming. *The Battle for Middle-earth: Tolkien's Divine Design in* The Lord of the Rings. Wm. B. Eerdmans Publishing, 2004.

Shippey, Tom. *J. R. R. Tolkien: Author of the Century.* HarperCollins, 2000.

———. *The Road to Middle-earth: How J. R. R. Tolkien Created a New Mythology.* Houghton Mifflin Books, 2003.

Smol, Anna. "'Oh…oh…Frodo!': Readings of Male Intimacy in *The Lord of the Rings.*" *MFS Modern Fiction Studies*, vol. 50, 2004, pp. 949–79, doi.org/10.1353/mfs.2005.0010.

Snyder, Mark, and Dave Smith. "Personality and Friendship: The Friendship Worlds of Self-Monitoring." *Friendship and Social Interaction*, edited by V. J. Derlega and B. A. Winstead, Springer, 1986, pp. 63–80, doi.org/10.1007/978-1-4612-4880-4_4.

St. Clair, Gloriana. "*The Lord of the Rings* as Saga." *Mythlore*, vol. 6, no. 2, 15 Apr. 1979, pp. 11–16, dc.swosu.edu/mythlore/vol6/iss2/3.

Stoddard, William. "A Critical Approach to Fantasy with Application to *The Lord of the Rings.*" *Mythlore*, vol. 10, no. 3, 1984, pp. 8–13, dc.swosu.edu/mythlore/vol10/iss3/3.

Strauss, Valeria. "The Importance of a Name." *The Washington Post*, 19 Sept 2014, www.washingtonpost.com/news/answer-sheet/wp/2014/09/19/the-importance-of-a-name/.

Taylor, Charles. *A Secular Age.* Harvard UP, 2007.

Tolkien, J. R. R. *The Annotated Hobbit: The Hobbit, or There and Back Again.* Annotated by Douglas A. Anderson, Houghton Mifflin, 2002.

———. *The Letters of J. R. R. Tolkien.* Edited by Humphrey Carpenter with the assistance of Christopher Tolkien, Houghton Mifflin Company, 2000.

———. *The Lord of the Rings.* Houghton Mifflin Harcourt, 2004.

———. *Sauron Defeated: The End of the Third Age (The History of* The Lord of the Rings *Part Four)* The History of Middle-earth Volume 9. Edited by Christopher Tolkien, Houghton Mifflin, 1992.

———. *The Silmarillion.* 2nd ed., edited by Christopher Tolkien, Houghton Mifflin, 2001.

———. "Mythopoeia" *Tree and Leaf.* HarperCollins, 2001.

———. "On Fairy-stories" *Tree and Leaf.* HarperCollins, 2001.

———. *Unfinished Tales of Númenor and Middle-earth.* Edited by Christopher Tolkien, Houghton Mifflin, 1980.

Valente, Claire. "Translating Tolkien's Epic: Peter Jackson's *Lord of the Rings*." *Intercollegiate Review*, vol. 40, no. 1, 2004, pp. 35–43, www.proquest.com/docview/210675496.

Waito, David M. "The Shire Quest: The 'Scouring of the Shire' as the Narrative and Thematic Focus of *The Lord of the Rings*." *Mythlore*, vol. 28, no. 3, 15 Apr. 2010, pp. 155–76, dc.swosu.edu/mythlore/vol28/iss3/11.

Walker, Stephen L. "The *War of the Rings* Treelogy: An Elegy for Lost Innocence and Wonder." *Mythlore*, vol. 5 no. 1, May 1978, pp. 3–5, dc.swosu.edu/mythlore/vol5/iss1/1.

Walker, Steve. *The Power of Tolkien's Prose: Middle-earth's Magical Style*. Palgrave Macmillan, 2009.

Weber, Max. "Science as a Vocation." *The Vocation Lectures*, edited by David S. Owen and Tracy B. Strong, translated by Rodney Livingstone, Hackett Publishing, 2004, pp. 1–31.

West, Richard C. "The Interlace Structure of *The Lord of the Rings*." *A Tolkien Compass*, edited by Jared Lobdell, Ballantine Books, 1975, pp. 82–102.

Williams, John T. "Conflict Theory and Race Conflict." *Social Science*, vol. 51, no. 1, 1976, pp. 32–36. www.jstor.org/stable/41886040.

Wordsworth, William. *Selected Poems*. Edited with an introduction and notes by Stephen Gill, Penguin Classics, 2004.

Yandell, Stephen. "'A Pattern Which Our Nature Cries Out For': The Medieval Tradition of the Ordered Four in the Fiction of J. R. R. Tolkien." *Mythlore*, vol. 21, no. 2, Oct. 1996, dc.swosu.edu/mythlore/vol21/iss2/57.

Zador, Anthony M. "A Critique of Pure Learning and What Artificial Neural Networks Can Learn from Animal Brains." *Nature Communications*, vol. 10, 2019, doi.org/10.1038/s41467-019-11786-6.

Acknowledgments

We cannot adequately express our gratitude to everyone who made this work possible. Although there were only nine in this fellowship, it took a much broader community to complete this project. We would like to thank our wonderful mentors who lent us their expertise and insight: Mary R. Bowman, Christopher Noble, Devin Brown, Tom Shippey, Steven Smith, Patrick Curry, Caleb Spencer, Mary K. Ducey, Woody Wendling, Carl F. Hostetter, Susan Wendling, Thomas Honegger, and Steve Yandell. Janet Brennan Croft was also a key mentor in this research and graciously wrote the foreword.

We would also like to thank David Bratman for his detailed notes and his thoughtful work in indexing the manuscript. Barbara Hayes was also essential in her careful attention while proofreading. We are grateful to the artists who worked with us during this journey, including Lily Rene Johnson, Zoe Zeimis, Caedon Spilman, and Megan Kornreich. We would also like to acknowledge David Weeks in his vision and support of this project from its inception.

Heartfelt thanks to the entire team at Mythopoeic Press for their hard work, vision, and tireless support, especially for their quick response, thoughtful critique, and brilliant attention to detail. The Mythopoeic Press shows an unflagging commitment to excellence in scholarship. They lead the field, and we are truly grateful.

Finally, we would like to thank our family and friends for their loving support and unrelenting attention to our work. It would not be what it is without you. We, as authors, would not be the people we are today without you. Thank you for journeying back with us, again and again. We hope you leave feeling as intrigued and inspired as we have every step of the way.

About the Contributors

Jacob Bradley is a lover of fantasy and how the stories we tell can shape our own. He graduated from Azusa Pacific University with a BS in International Business and Honors Humanities with a minor in Spanish and now directs operations at Summit Community Church in Buckeye, Arizona.

Britta E. Bunnel is a Tolkien enthusiast who holds a BS in Biology and Honors Humanities from Azusa Pacific University. Currently, she is pursuing a Medical Degree at Washington State University's Elson S. Floyd College of Medicine. Britta aspires to serve communities holistically through medicine, combining what she loves about science with her passion for building relationships.

Janet Brennan Croft (ORCiD 0001-0001-2691-3586) is an Associate University Librarian at the University of Northern Iowa. She is the author of *War in the Works of J. R. R. Tolkien* (Praeger, 2004; winner, Mythopoeic Society Award for Inklings Studies). She has also written on the Peter Jackson Middle-earth films, the Whedonverse, *Orphan Black*, J. K. Rowling, Terry Pratchett, Lois McMaster Bujold, *The Devil Wears Prada*, and other authors, TV shows, and movies. She is editor or co-editor of many collections of literary essays, the most recent being *Loremasters and Libraries in Fantasy and Science Fiction: A Gedenkschrift for David Oberhelman*, co-edited with Jason Fisher (Mythopoeic Press, 2022). She edits the refereed scholarly journal *Mythlore* and is archivist and assistant editor of *Slayage: The International Journal of Buffy+*. You can follow her work on Academia.edu.

Anna K. Dickinson holds BAs in Communication Studies and Spanish along with a major in Honors Humanities from Azusa Pacific University. Her love of stories has given her a deep appreciation for great literature and a desire to pursue a career as a therapist. To realize that desire, she is working toward an MS in Marriage and Family Therapy from Fuller Theological Seminary.

Diana Pavlac Glyer teaches in the Honors College at Azusa Pacific University. She is an award-winning author: her book *The Company They Keep: C. S. Lewis and J. R. R. Tolkien as Writers in Community* changed the way we talk about these writers. *Bandersnatch: C. S. Lewis, J. R. R. Tolkien, and the Creative Collaboration of the Inklings* shows us how to follow in their footsteps. Her scholarship, her teaching, and her work as an artist all circle back to one common theme: creativity thrives in community.

Joshua Harbman is passionately interdisciplinary. He earned a BS in Applied Mathematics complemented by a major in Honors Humanities from Azusa Pacific University. He has always enjoyed the dynamic interplay between complex technical studies and deeply creative work. He is now working at Waymo LLC on autonomous driving technology while carving out time to read, write, and dwell on ideas of beauty.

Mark E. Jung has been inspired by the ways leaders foster community and hopes to do the same. He graduated from Azusa Pacific University with a BA in Business Management and Honors Humanities. Currently, Mark works in Public Affairs at Kaiser Permanente and enjoys the unique stories told through books, sports, and movies.

Jensen A. Kirkendall is an independent scholar with an MA in English from Wake Forest University and a BA in English and Honors Humanities from Azusa Pacific University. His areas of interest include Victorian poetry and fairy tales, Great Works education, the fantastic throughout different literary eras, the history of ideas, and disenchantment. He currently lives and works at a local bakeshop in Winston-Salem, North Carolina. He enjoys gardening, bouldering, poetry, and teaching classes at his church.

Jordan F. Mar received a BS in Biology and Honors Humanities from Azusa Pacific University and is currently on a journey toward a DDS degree at Loma Linda University. When she is not studying health sciences, she enjoys learning about great works of literature, social dynamics, and spiritual growth. Like Samwise, she loves cooking, exchanging stories, and joining friends on ordinary and extraordinary adventures.

About the Contributors

Hana Paz earned an Interdisciplinary BA in Global Studies and Teaching English to Speakers of Other Languages, enhanced by her Honors Humanities major. She has long pondered the problem of evil in our world and has been moved to pursue paths that center around supporting those who have experienced evils such as displacement, isolation, and abandonment. Currently, she is developing her path of vocation through a career in social work and is interested in continuing her scholarship on the influence of evil through the studies of trauma-informed care and practical theology.

Wyatt Zeimis is an avid reader of fantasy and science-fiction. He earned a BS in Computer Science and Honors Humanities at Azusa Pacific University, which offered a complimentary blend of his analytical skills and his interest in philosophy. His love for novelty and nature leads him to explore the world and connect with other people through frequent travels and outdoor excursions.

Index

Alberto, Maria 68
Alfred, King 99
alliances 46–47
animals 21–23
Aragorn: confessor to Boromir 60–62; displaying enchantment 119; healer 26–27, 62–63, 119; as hero 28–29; leader 59, 63–64, 78–79; lore-master 18; lover of Arwen 18, 51–52; mentee of Gandalf 50; merciful judge of Beregond 93–94, 95; name 16, 38, 113; has premonitions 98n81; revelation of character 15–17; steward 58–59; as Strider 62; not viewpoint character 11
Arendt, Hannah 18–19
Aristotle 45
Ar-Pharazôn 117–18, 121
Arwen 18, 51–52
Augustine of Hippo, St. 71–72, 74n65, 75

battles 10, 30–32, 92
Bauman, Zygmunt 111, 117
Beregond: companion to Pippin 8, 79; saves Faramir 31n34, 93; judged by Aragorn 93–94, 95
Beren 18, 52
Bergil 8, 9
Bilbo Baggins: birthday party 109; helped by eagles 97; relationship with Frodo 38–39, 40n42, 135n128; pity towards Gollum 88, 92, 105; as Ring-bearer 100
Black Riders *see* Nazgûl
Boethius 99
Boromir: his dream 98–99, 100; his failure and redemption 60–62, 64, 75, 80–81
Branchaw, Sherrylyn 62

Caldecott, Stratford 27–28, 33, 41
Carpenter, Humphrey 30, 86
Celeborn 118, 130
chance 100–02, 114. *see also* hope, providence
Chance, Jane 29, 30, 35, 57–58
Chesterton, G. K. 121
Cicero 45–46, 47
civilization 114, 118
coincidence 97, 101, 114

Confucius 40
Croft, Janet Brennan i–ii, 113

darkness 71, 75–76
Denethor: as corrupted goodness 74, 75, 82; irony of his despair 13–14, 110n88; isolation as Steward and father 40, 58, 74; misperception of Pippin 35; suicide 93
Detienne, Marcel 118
disenchantment 109–11, 114–16, 120–22
Donnelly, Colleen 57, 58
dreams 98–99, 100
Drúedain 127–28
Drury, Rogery 101
Dubs, Kathleen E. 99–100
Dwarves 42–45, 117

eagles 97, 107
Elrond 31, 73, 101, 110
Elves 19n26, 42–44, 99, 112
enchantment 22–23, 109–21. *see also The Lord of the Rings*: value and quality of; recovery
Ents 14, 19, 130–32
Éomer 16, 79, 92, 119
Éowyn: in disguise 31n34; love of Aragorn 58–59; love of Théoden 39, 40; slaying of the Nazgûl 9–10
Evans, G. R. 72, 73
evil: confrontation with 32, 106, 132; as corrupted goodness 73–76; lessons for readers 81–83; weight of 77–80
evil, Augustinian (privative, as non-being) 69–76
evil, Manichaean (dualistic) 67–69, 72, 75–76

family relationships 32–33, 37–40
Faramir: dream 98–99; healing by Aragorn 62; at Henneth Annûn 90, 102; love of Boromir 39
fellowship i, 137–38
Fellowship of the Ring: breaking of 12; formation and connection 47, 53, 101; on their Quest 15, 20, 60–61, 102; qualities of 67–68
Fili 39–40
Fimi, Dimitra 43
Flieger, Verlyn 28, 124, 129, 131
foresight 98–100
friendship 37, 40–49, 53–54, 68; cross-cultural 42–44; intergenerational 44; of utility 45–46
Frodo Baggins: friendships 41; with Bilbo 38–39, 135n128; with Fellowship 47–48; with Sam 29–30, 48–50, 81; as hero 29; as hobbit 27–28; last journey as recovery 135; perception of Aragorn 16; perspective of 13; providence and 102–03; as Ring-bearer 34n39, 105–06, 123; and with Boromir 60–61, 75; and with Gollum 47–48, 88–91, 94–95; forgiveness of Gollum 86n74; reactions to landscape 19–20

Index

Galadriel: gifts of 103–05, 135; Mirror 99–100; understanding with Gimli 43
Gandalf: as background mover of events 13; on chance and providence 100, 102–03, 110; and Denethor 58, 93; and enchantment 111–12; hope in response to evil 81–83; lore-master 18n23, 130; mentor to Aragorn 50; to hobbits 30; perspective of 8; on pity and mercy for Gollum 86, 88; for Wormtongue 92–93; his return 133–34
Garth, John 30, 49
Ghân-buri-Ghân 127–28
Gildor 78
Gimli: friendship with Legolas 42–44; in the Paths of the Dead 10–11
Glyer, Diana Pavlac i–iv, 41, 137–38
Gollum: character 85–86; good comes from evil 82; history and role in the story 88–92, 105–06; as Ring-bearer and with Frodo 47–48, 94–95; as subject of pity 80
Gondor 46, 60–61, 63, 74–75
goodness 68, 83, 105; loss of 73–75
Greenwood, Linda 61
grief 19, 51, 86n74

Hammond, Wayne G. 63, 91, 130
heroism 28–32, 61, 97. *see also* leadership
Hick, John 72, 73
Hirsch, Bernhard 32n36, 33n38
Hobbit, The (Tolkien): family relationship of Fili and Kili to Thorin 39–40. Scenes: Bilbo and Gollum (ch. 5) 88–89, 105; Thorin's deathbed speech (ch. 18) 26
Hobbits 27–28, 44, 131–32; experiences with Men 126–28; family relationships 38; overlooked 35
homosexuality 49n48
Honegger, Thomas 40n42
hope 79, 80–83; and despair 58, 63–64, 71. *see also* chance, providence
Hopkins, Gerard Manley 112n92
Houghton, John Wm. 72, 75

Isildur 59, 118n104

Keesee, Neal K. 72
Kilby, Clyde S. 17
Kili 39–40
Kisor, Yvette 70
Kreeft, Peter 68, 101–02

landscape 19–21
Langford, Jonathan D. 31n34, 127
Latour, Bruno 115
leadership 57–64; hobbits in 135; mastership 48–50; mentorship 50; restoration of 59–60
Legolas 10, 42–44, 134

Lewis, C. S.: on enchantment 120; on family 38, 40; on friendship 40–41, 41–42, 49n48, 53–54; on story vii, 12; *The Voyage of the Dawn Treader* 116n101

Lord of the Nazgûl 82 *see also* slaying of *under* Lord of the Rings: Scenes, Book V

Lord of the Rings, The (Tolkien): capitalization of words 86; coda of 32n36; depth of 15–17; function of stories in 1–2; narrative techniques 5–6, 27; narrative threads (interlace) 12–14, 106; paragraph breaks 10n9, 79; perspectives and focalization in 7–11, 25, 35, 45; as a reading experience 138–39; realism of fantasy in 2, 120; sequel to *The Hobbit* 21–22; supporting characters 8n6; value and quality of iii, 2–3, 5, 123

  Scenes, Book I: Sam and Ted in the Green Dragon (ch. 2) 109; Gandalf and Frodo discuss the past (ch. 2) 88, 100, 105–06; the fox (ch. 3) 5–6, 21–22; first encounter with the Nazgûl (ch. 3) 123, 133; Gildor (ch. 3) 78; Farmer Maggot (ch. 4) 34; Bucklebury Ferry (ch. 4) 133; Crickhollow (ch. 5) 41; The Old Forest (in general) (ch. 6) 19; Old Man Willow (ch. 6) 100–01, 113, 129–30; the house of Tom Bombadil (ch. 7) 1–2; the Barrow-wights (ch. 8) 104–05; the Prancing Pony (ch. 10) 16; Aragorn treats Frodo's injury (ch. 12) 62

  Scenes, Book II: Council of Elrond (ch. 2) 73, 101; Boromir's dream (ch. 2) 98–99, 100; Gandalf's tale of Saruman (ch. 2) 82, 110–12, 113; forming of the Fellowship (ch. 3) 31; the stones of Hollin (ch. 3) 19; Mirrormere (ch. 6) 19; Cerin Amroth (ch. 6) 16; the Fellowship meet Galadriel (ch. 7) 43; the Mirror of Galadriel (ch. 7) 99, 100; Celeborn bids the Fellowship farewell (ch. 8) 118, 130; the Argonath (ch. 9) 16, 113; the fall of Boromir (ch. 10) 60, 75; Frodo on Amon Hen (ch. 10) 13, 102–03

  Scenes, Book III: the redemption of Boromir (ch. 1) 60–62; the breaking of the Fellowship (ch. 1) 12–13); the Three Hunters meet the Riders of Rohan (ch. 2) 13, 16–17, 119; Pippin drops the brooch (ch. 3) 104; Merry and Pippin escape the orcs (ch. 3) 103; they meet Treebeard (ch. 4) 44, 112, 125, 131–32; Treebeard's lament (ch. 4) 80; the Three Hunters in Fangorn (ch. 5) 14; the return of Gandalf (ch. 5) 13, 133–34; Théoden's pity towards Wormtongue (ch. 6) 59–60, 92, 95; the Battle of Helm's Deep (ch. 8) 43, 103; the Glittering Caves (ch. 8) 43; Pippin and the palantír (ch. 11) 7–8; a Nazgûl flies overhead (ch. 11) 77–78

  Scenes, Book IV: the taming of Sméagol (ch. 1) 47–48, 89–90; the Dead Marshes (ch. 2) 20; Sam sees the Southron (ch. 4) 126–27; Henneth Annûn (ch. 5) 39, 102; the Forbidden Pool (ch. 6) 90; the stairs of Cirith Ungol (ch. 8) 20; Gollum finds Frodo asleep (ch. 8) 94–95; the Phial of Galadriel in Cirith Ungol (ch. 10) 104

  Scenes, Book V: Gandalf and Pippin in Denethor's hall (ch. 1) 35, 58, 82; Pippin with Beregond and Bergil (ch. 1) 8–9, 79; the Paths of the Dead (ch. 2) 10–11, 58–59; the Riding of the Dead (ch. 2) 99; the Riding of the Rohirrim (ch. 3) 46–47; Gandalf and Pippin under the siege of Gondor (ch. 4) 82; Pippin asks Beregond to save Faramir (ch. 4) 93; Drúadan Forest (ch. 5) 125, 127–28; the slaying of the Lord of the Nazgûl (ch. 6) 9–10, 31, 70–71, 105; Éomer at the Battle of the Pelennor Fields (ch. 6) 79; the pyre of Denethor (ch. 7) 74; the Houses of Healing (ch. 8) 26–27, 41–42, 62–63, 119; the Host of the West marches to the Black Gate (ch. 10) 63–64, 78–79

Scenes, Book VI: Sam as Ring-bearer (ch. 1) 78; Sam sings of Western Lands (ch. 1) 81; ascent of Mount Doom (ch. 3) 25–26, 49–50; Sammath Naur (ch. 3) 85, 91, 95, 106; Fall of Mordor (ch. 3) 71; rescue by the eagles (ch. 4) 97, 107; crowning of Aragorn (ch. 5) 50; Aragorn judges Beregond (ch. 5) 93–94, 95; the Scouring of the Shire (ch. 8) 31–32, 34n39, 134–35; Sam uses Galadriel's gift (ch. 9) 20, 105, 135; Frodo to the Grey Havens (ch. 9) 39; "Well, I'm back" (ch. 9) 33

 Other sections of: Prologue 27; Tale of Aragorn and Arwen (Appx. A.I (v)) 51–52; Durin's Folk (Appx. A.III) 117; Epilogue 33n37

Lord of the Rings movies 85n73
Lore-masters 18–19
Lothlórien 19–20, 112
Lowentrout, Peter 114–15, 121
Luling, Virginia 114, 118, 119n105
Lúthien 18, 52

Maggot, Farmer 34
magic 99, 109, 112–13
master-servant relationship 48–50, 57, 91
Men, as a people 10n10, 19n26, 126–28
mentorship ii, 50
mercy 49, 59–60, 67, 86–96; definition 87–88
Merry Brandybuck: courage and heroism 31–32; in Drúadan Forest 127; friendships 41–42, 44; in the Old Forest 129; and restoration of the Shire 135–36; and slaying of the Lord of the Nazgûl 9–11, 104–05
Minas Tirith 8–9
Mordor 20, 28
Morgoth 68–69
Moseley, Charles 6
"Mythopoeia" (Tolkien) 68, 69, 77, 115–16

names 112–13, 132; epithets 63, 113; lineage 16, 38; Sméagol-Gollum 89–90, 94–95
nature iii, 111n91, 128–32
Nazgûl: as evil beings 70–71, 72–73; fate of 82; fear incited by 77–78, 133; origin of 75n67. *See also* slaying of the Lord of the Nazgûl *under Lord of the Rings: Scenes, Book V*
Northrup, Clyde B. 28
Númenor 116–18
Nussbaum, Martha C. 6n3

objects, useful and valued 26–27, 103–05
Old Man Willow 1, 129
One Ring: history 100; as object of fear 78; peril of 60, 75, 89n75. *see also individual Ring–bearers*
"On Fairy-stories" (Tolkien) 17, 119–20

Partridge, Christopher 111
Pippin Took: courage and heroism 31–32; friendships 41–42; with Treebeard 44,

131; in Minas Tirith 8–9, 35, 79, 93; and palantír 7–8; and restoration of the Shire 135–36
pity 49, 59–60, 80, 85–95; definition 86–88
precious, as descriptor 25n29
providence 97–107, 110. *see also* chance, hope

quest: distractions 78, 85–86; events during 13–15, 20, 25, 34, 133; nature of 5, 19, 123; priorities 60–61; purpose 27–28, 88–92, 102–03, 105–06; relationships in 52; strategy 63; value 21–23, 31–32

racism 43–44
recovery i, 5, 119–20, 124–26, 132–34; novelty of the familiar 125–26, 134–36. *see also* enchantment
relationships ii, 32–33, 37–54, 68, 91
Ring *see* One Ring
Ringwraiths *see* Nazgûl
Rutledge, Fleming 94, 100

Sam (Samwise) Gamgee: and Galadriel's gifts 104–05; and Gollum 89–92, 94–95; as hero 29–30; has hope in Mordor 81; longing for enchantment 109; lore-master 18n23; and magic 112; experiences with Men (Aragorn, the Southron) 126–27; relationship with Frodo 48–50; and restoration of the Shire 134–35; return to normal life 33; as Ring-bearer 78; useful objects (his cookware) 25–26
Saruman: as corrupted goodness 74, 75; corruptor and destroyer 32, 80, 132–35; disenchantment of 109–11, 121; names 113
Sauron: as evil 67, 73–75; Eye and will of 13, 102–03; influence of 8, 110; in Númenor 117
Scull, Christina 63, 91, 130
Serkis, Andy 85n73
Shelob 75–76, 104
Shippey, Tom 13, 14, 29, 77, 123
Shire, The 31–32, 39, 105, 134–36
Silmarillion, The (Tolkien): as background to *The Lord of the Rings* 17n20; falls of Melkor and Sauron 74n62.
    Scenes: Ainulindalë 68–69; the two trees of Valinor (Quenta ch. 1) 128n119; Ungoliant (Quenta ch. 8) 75–76; origin and fate of Men (Quenta ch. 12) 10n10, 19n26; Beren and Lúthien (Quenta ch. 19) 18, 22, 52; Fall of Númenor (Akallabêth) 116–18
stewardship 57–59, 64, 74, 132
sub-creation 17n19, 124
symbiotic connections 45–48

Taylor, Charles 114
Théoden: in Drúadan Forest 127–28; love of Éowyn 39; last words 10; as leader 31, 59–60; pity towards Wormtongue 92–93, 95
Thorin Oakenshield 26, 39–40
Tolkien, Christopher 17n20, 98
Tolkien, Edith 52

Index

Tolkien, J. R. R.: Catholicism 87; development of his legendarium 17–18; on enchantment 115–16; on evil 68, 72, 74n65, 77; on family relationships 38; friendships 41; love of nature iii, 111n91, 128; love for wife Edith 52; on love and romance 51; on providence 98, 106; on recovery and escape 119–21, 124–25; writing process 14–15; in World War I 26, 33n38, 49; and World Wars 77
Tom Bombadil: on chance and providence 101; on Farmer Maggot 34; as master 129; and names 113; storyteller 1–2
Treebeard: character, 130–32; friendship with hobbits 44; laments 80; and names 112, 132; on Saruman 111
trees 111n91, 128–32
trolls 76

Ungoliant 75–76
Unlight 75–76

Valar 19n26, 98–99, 117

Walker, Steve 21
Weber, Max 110
Williams, Charles 32
Witch-king *see* slaying of the Lord of the Nazgûl *under* Lord of the Rings: Scenes, Book V
Wormtongue 59, 92–93, 95

Yandell, Stephen 7n5

Made in the USA
Las Vegas, NV
20 November 2022